ñandutí: weaving into the crocheteried m

ñandutí lace: ñandutimichí:

ñi-fleur that my needle pursues with

excruciating patience for hours and

hours is hand-stitching se

slowly off the fluctuating se

er du soleil that set uleur

automne of now: here ñandu pa

of feeling: je m'assois: je me sens:

ñandu: being a cancer my verb is self...

o sense or feel: me voir: ñandu: winte

ore than automne panique automn

ñandu: what is the secret d'identité ent

hese deux things absolument distincte

spiders and scorpions? : yes, scorpior

of the heart: ñandu: they alight and stir

you, pincent you with all they've go

he ñandu jolt mortally occurring: mea

Paraguayan Sea

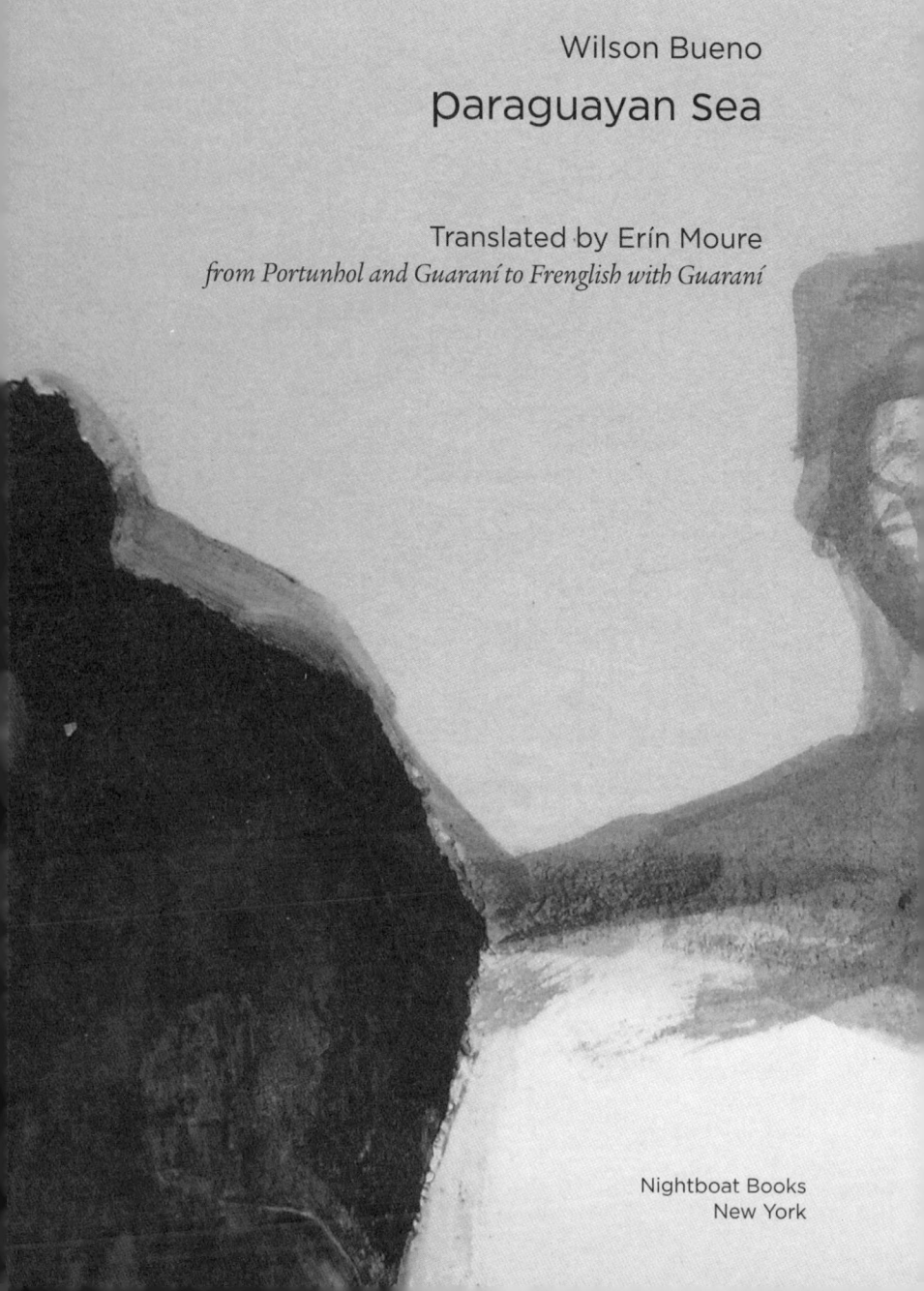

Wilson Bueno

Paraguayan Sea

Translated by Erín Moure
from Portunhol and Guaraní to Frenglish with Guaraní

Nightboat Books
New York

Mar Paraguayo by Wilson Bueno © 1992 by Wilson Bueno
First published by Editora Iluminuras Ltda, São Paulo, Brazil
All other original texts © the authors
All translations © 2017 Erín Moure
All rights reserved
Printed in the United States

ISBN 978-1-937658-74-8

Design and typesetting by Margaret Tedesco
Endpapers designed by Andrew Forster
Text set in Gotham and ITC Legacy
Cover and interior art: Vida Simon: *Whobody's Lure*, 2008

Cataloging-in-publication data is available
from the Library of Congress

Distributed by University Press of New England
One Court Street
Lebanon, NH 03766
www.upne.com

Nightboat Books
New York
www.nightboat.org

Contents & Contentments

Contents

Contentments

Paraguayan Soup

Original introduction by Néstor Perlongher, São Paulo, 1992; translated and intertweeted from Spanish

Paraguayan Sea, by Wilson Bueno, is an exceptional event, of the kind usually so quiet they are almost imperceptible, detected only by those in the know. But once they settle, once they claim their place, it's as if the place had always been theirs. Everything's the same yet, subtly, all is altered. The event pokes holes in our habits, and in the rhythms of the cosmos; its perturbations are tinged with an indescribable glint of the irreversible, of the definitive.

In this case, the event involves the *invention* of a language. Imitation and invention, says Gabriel Tarde, are the greatest of human passions (practices). Maybe it was Wilson Bueno who actually "invented" Portunhol—a Portunhol dappled by Guaraní deployed from beneath, in the pulsing marrow of the language, just as Argentinian (or Correntine) poet Francisco Madariaga invoked it from above in his luxuriously humidly surrealist *gaucho-Bedouin-Afro-Hispanic-Guaraní.* Or else, from his artistic *Altazor,* Bueno plucked it out, or snitched it from small talk, warm bowl of maté in hand and the gringa topping it up from the pot, outside in wicker chairs in the yard behind the kitchen. He plucked it in Spanish and Portuguese, let it go in one ear and not out of the other. It might seem a stretch but Wilson Bueno has something of Manuel Puig, whose writings, rooted in conversation, also shoot the breeze, and something of the chronicler as well, because he collects a parlance that is fairly widespread: almost all Spanish speakers in Brazil express themselves in this inconsistent, precarious and fickle mix of languages.

The motley mixture is not structured as a predetermined code of signification; it's faithful only to its own capriciousness, deviance and error.

Portunhol is immediately poetic. Between the two major languages, there's a vacillation, a tension, a constant oscillation: one is, at once, the "error" of the other and its possible destiny, uncertain and improbable. A singular fascination arises from this clash of deviances (as a linguist with a legal bent might say). There's no rule of law: there's grammar but it's unruly; there's spelling, but it's erratic: *chuva* and *lluvia* in Spanish and Portuguese (spelled whichever way) coexist in the same paragraph, to mention but one of innumerable examples.

As aberrant mixture, *Paraguayan Sea* is akin to *Paraguayan Soup*, a dish that, contrary to expectations, does not invite a soup spoon, but is a kind of *sui generis* omelet or corn pone. The waves of the *Sea* are tottering: who knows where they'll topple; they lack harbor and itinerary; everything in them bobs in baroque suspension between prose and poetry, becoming-animal and becoming-woman.

Out of the breadth of this blooming *Paraguayan Sea*—which recalls an epic poem by the Argentinian Romantic Esteban Echeverría taught to us in school, "incommensurable, open and mysterious from head to toe"—poetry spies us, leaps on us like a puppy—the microscopic Brinks—sometimes playful, sometimes savage. Random poetry, for some critics would say it appears casually, without determination in the indeterminate. It's useful to remember, for example, that in Spanish *sin* is not the Portuguese *sim*, it's *sem:* not *yes* but *without,* thus withdrawing the assertion of its existence. And something infinitely comic guffaws in Bueno's replacement of *son* by *san*, of *they are* by *saint.*

A continual hilarity, unprovoked and born naturally from the linguistic amalgam, marks Bueno's disquieting text. An avant-garde experience, the text can be compared to *Catatau* by Paulo Leminski (significantly, also from Paraná) and, even more daringly, to Julián Ríos's *Larva*: they all play with language, inventing and reinventing it. But whereas *Catatau* rests on the high culture that impregnates its subtext despite collapses, destructions and reconstructions, Bueno's book is founded on a pathetic burst of laughter, the tragicomedy of everyday agonies incarnated in the slippage of languages, one of those tragic soap operas that ends badly if at all, though one with more density, depth: it may seem entertaining but is no entertainment.

The merit of *Paraguayan Sea* lies precisely in the microscopic and molecular labor within its galloping inter-languages (or inter-rivers), within its indeterminations which function as a *minor language* (to echo Deleuze and Guattari) that mines the preposterous majesty of major languages, through which it wanders as if without intention, without system, completely untimely and surprising, like good poetry, never predictable. The tale is like Bueno's Guaratuban floozy or *catin* who, in giving her dog kilometrically diminutive nicknames (blossoms plucked from Guaraní that irrupt to intensify the poetic temperature of the tale), extends the microscopia of its canine grandeur, to attract and seduce us with the motion of its bifurcated tail, as if it were mermaid pretending to be manatee, or manatee mimicking mermaid, until the sprinkled glitter of its scaly tail drowns us in the iridescent ecstasy of a vast, deep sea.

How, finally, to read *Paraguayan Sea?* Those with an obsession for plot (which exists but its matter is indecisive and entangled, thanks to its porous composition) who ignore the poetic evolutions and mutations of its language will miss out, like those readers of (badly) translated pulp novels who gravitate toward half-digested plot resumés. *Paraguayan Sea* may be a torrid tale, but it can't be turned into a tweet!

AVIS

Make no mistake: Guaraní is as essential to this story as the flight of the birrd, the speck on the window, the cooing of French or the cascade of Nerudaesque outpourings in a single seule suicide of capacious English words. One's the error of the autre. Maybe I wanted at times to end up ingesting, in this zoo of signes, the essential curl of sensation in the tail of le scorpion. Just this: I was désirant of all that vibrates and buzzes beneath, far beneath the ligne of silence. Il n'y a pas de langages là. Only the vertige de language. It tells me I existe. And because of this I will chante my marafona floozy song aloud along the beaches of Guaratuba, forbidden by the oldguy who drags his butt around the house like a pale being gone cold, suffering the oldguy's acts as necessary evil—never killing him despite my efforts to endure nights and days of pure abuse in a macabre obsession with tricking his grizzled neckskin. No, believeyoume, I speak truly: I didn't kill the oldie.

And then there was le boy with his thighs clenched hard—concocted strength of men in his shoulders and in the obsessive meat of his sex with which obsessively he seeks and hunts me: me his prisonnière and chasseur.

Ñe'ẽ.

I'm the *catin* trollop of this beach town, a marafona floozy.[1] Ici, in Guaratuba, I survive by my wits. Ah, and my happiness is divine before the sun, that crystal balle charged with the futur like a bomb that will explose the uranium of the day. My sea. The sea.[2] Merde la vie that je porte on my back like a madame très digne strut-tutt to the guillotine. Oh, God have it... Ouai, there's God and there's my gob. What can anyone do?

Today I see myself in the eyebeam of his dead yeux, that man who made me jitter like castanets between the sheets, who made me suffrir, who made a me, qui m'a construit out of agony and blood, le blood-drip shed by my bitter life. From his shoulders, my destiny like a fate faite with a dagger in the right chambre of the heart.

1 Doll and not doll, faceless and facing, hey Dolly! (EM)

2 A-fluent sea, a fluency. (EM)

Right this minute now, I'm gobsmacked, in front of his grim face, sunken red eyes, those eyes that were my eyes.

No, I didn't kill him because his vie was caught up en mine. It was destiné pure, I tell you. My fortuitous divination of la draw, in meteoroid and crystal ball: avant tout I saw him plus mort que la dead.

I was born deep in the deepest rural depths of my country—on a Guaraní ranch, all Guarania and solitude. The first time I'ai approché the sea, there was only see in sight of sea—my gaze so charged with waves and bleu. Besides, I carried deep in moi an entirely other chanson—stuck in the elevator, despair, suicidal desperations and sourness.

I had no fear of the huge abyss of eau d'sea et foam. It held my stare, though tout ce que I felt was girlish joie in the sun, moi who was already in its lure, with terreur et patches of grey hair, already lured to return yes to the Cape of Good Hope.

My body'd gone flaccid from being cooped up in that dark room where je trace le destin, or the fate, of the man whom my hands ont fini par suavely assassinating—in the guise of a swan or a sword. Or was it him who'd upped and died?

It was très simple: I just grabbed him unawares in un moment of distraction with the malevolence inherent in being his attendant and obligatory esclave, je l'ai jetté on the sofa avec terreur et fear—strangely muet and dans une solitude abrupt. No drip of blood to cause me problèmes, no, pas une seule goutte.

I pursue l'art of sorcery, ranch-style house with mangoes in the garden and shade trees in the yard, not to mention the sun, the harsh soleil morning, noon and night—the frightening summer of Guaratuba when c'est décembre in the southern hemisphère et all the world lounges under awnings and young guys traipse the beaches in afternoon light—what a great little artiste, the sky with its couleurs.

At night, I've my emploi: it's not that I fall in love, no, that's not it, what I have to say is such a labyrinth of spidery webs that spin high in the corners of the house, while I lounge in front of the télévision watching Sonîa Braga in the soap opera *Gabriela*—her thighs give me goosebumps whenever they appear on screen as if they were the ultimate aim of a life, my life, life—oh life on the flie.

I know he's dead as a doornail and that, dead, the oldguy will live forever stuck to my chest in the swelling memory of his tongue subtly exploiting me with gusto, pleasure and orgasm.

Each time I dream more and more of Braga, that Sônia of my floozy life, those deep blacks visible, seeing. Ah, here in the beach town of Guaratuba there's nobody, personne, no one who speaks my langue apart from the heavy silence of siestas calcinated by the height of summer, with cicadas agonized from singing and wee birds in the flamboyant treetops all giddy with l'été, a giddy laughter of pink dogwood beside the hibiscus that tells me it's already late, that it's already so late to be dying.

What an idea, what a crazy idea—j'oublie déjà, forget to tell you, sir, of the sole companion who lets me state, unerringly, that all this is as real as a hibiscus: my dog, my teensy-weensy pup who answers to the sound of Brinks and is so teenytiny, a furball, furry on top as if he were a bifurcated comma on the move.

Now for le drama. Añaretã. Añaretãmeguá.

Ever since the formation of these climats of smoke and anxiety of the soul, where does the fait of living come from, between prandials and prickles, claws and eggs so well shaped—shapes nearly births—of scorpions who emerge already into this world with their raw daggers? What am I talking about, these constant circumlocutions are a cabaret. I observe: here one arrives at supposed happiness, here or là, that toujours inachèvable felicité, and starts teasing girls, pulling up their jupes and skirts, putting fingers in the recesses of their proferred bodices.

Ñemomirĩhá. Ñemomirĩ. In my native tongue, things are smallest when they accrete with deaf ferocity. Ñemomirĩ. Ñemomirĩhá.

When I enter those quadrants of the magnificent mystère de l'existence, where the putrid exists, the sordid, the luxuriant, when I inflame myself like this nearly supreme, so many things start to churn again inside and so close to hell. Hell exists—maison of fire and flame, lamp lit in the depths of our scorched eyes.

Añaretãmeguá.

J'ai peur, j'ai beaucoup de fear of what might take place in le futur, of which there's so little here. It might be une miracle, might be l'abyss. Paraĩpĩeté is the total abyss of the sea.

La vérité est que je ne never know, and this makes me unfailingly afraid, without the least courage to go dehors dans la rue and promenade in my long muslin dresses, my necklaces, bracelets and the mother-of-pearl of my earrings. Et la fear is a viscous thing that comes from l'intérieur—lentement, extending hairy paws, approaching, subtly, to grab you, en panique, to grab you—irrevocably—by your heartstrings. Some, at that moment, just kill themselves. Añaretã that keeps moving. Dieu est-il mort? God, you say?

In the cabaret, I sit with the oldguy, me the floozy harlot of the beach of Guaratuba, and he orders, to commencer, un verre de minéral, but I note his eyes tremulous, note that the oldguy doesn't give a care about the prohibition la plus sévère of the doctor, our Doctor Paiva, who comes to see him once or twice a week. All the oldguy, le vieillard, cares about is that the nuit be drunken so as to chase me, to yank me, me, then, into bed, with his finitude plein de tremors and his sexe totalement impossible. Désir persists in the end like an amputated leg that keeps on itching. Añaretãmeguá?

Beneath hell there's only hell. Ceci I can dire without fear of a lie. Ma vie infirme, my floozy life of varicosities et cicatrices. La horloge by the window, the curtain shut, late nights of wine, moi dans this maison in the beach town of Guaratuba and le silence blunt breaking and flapping—drip by drip, insistent, recurring, presque dead. The danse enchantée des heures, ah quelle danse, yes sirree bob, without the soul of the round dance, the cururu, the cateretê, añaretãmeguá, la tupi-africaine danse in the shade, wandering error of the lugubrious, of moths or la pluie en les hivers de mon enfance of mud, of dust or of humid streets and of villages sans chance ni destination. Ancient house. My tava, my tavaiguá.

We're all frigging alone and that's the añaretã that lies lower than hell. We die and it's all scraped into hell. We take to the road, dark vagabonds on the byways, ruffians or gigolos, and there hell shows up, again and again et encore l'enfer. Hell. Añaretã. And wrinkles embed in your face and your hair turns white, grizzled, et this too is the stuff of l'enfer. The skin of God, these stones: tupaitá.

L'enfer, hell, añaretã, exists and is set against the sea, the sky, les wee mornings rich in sun and sparrows, fruit-laden mangos, given that l'enfer exists, añaretã, añaretãmenguá, and is self-sufficient—in the pull of its courants de hard steel and hunger. Yes, hunger for love and affection, but hunger so scandalous that it walks on shards of glass—barefoot and stark naked. Yarobi. It's the danse in the abyss of those adept at walking tightropes, or so I was told, years ago, in coarse Spanish, by my grand-mère argentine, throwing me the bitter taste of a failure, another nod, again and de nouveau, at the inexplicable matters of the heart. Is reason on the right or the left? What raison propels that muscle de flesh and blood and thorns?

If it weren't for my *catin* floozy life, the day'd draw to a close with préparatifs for supper for les kids, with the gentle anticipation of mothers who await their husbands, garnishing the meal so lovingly with a tomato cut into flower petals and set in mayonnaise; if it weren't for my floozy life I'd be the same as the others, the same as all of them, all those women full of joie and who only run for help from doctors, never psychiatres, and who only go when their blood pressure hits the roof. Ah, what a hard way to live. Ah, tecové, tecovemiki, tecovepá.

And so I brush, sometimes and souvent, against the mouvement de leur existence that, absurdly, even if we don't aspire to it, approaches the hell of embers et cleaver. Hell, añaretã, exists and we have to find a fugitive and vagabond façon to fool it, since it's alive in the serpent, mboi, mboihovĩ,[3] coral coral mboichumbé, and so we have to trick it as it arrives with its ferocious appetite, its bellow, it's beaucoup, it's like the whistle of bats, the chauvesouris: andĩrá, I don't even want to know how stupid, andĩrá, the ears incapable of hearing, andĩrá, the changeable and modular soundings of the bats that draw closer, morbidbat messengers of what hell is and they know, folks, they know all of it, hell existes and is very much innumerable. Right up to the rose in the rose in the Guimarães Rosa, karai.

When I threw him, the oldguy, onto the sofa, I was dreamy and useless, caught in one of those somnambulisms that take hold of me in excessive heat, a désir in the womb that sets sea aflame, cuñá, cuñambatará, embers of my sex boiling with the sins of

3   Refers to "Cobra Norato," epic poem by Raúl Bopp (1931). References to the cobra are references to gender ambiguity as well as to the ambiguity of the Guaraní color that is simultaneously (to Europeans) blue and green. (ref: Nádia Nelziza Lovera de Florentino, *Entre Gêneros e Fronteiras: uma leitura de Mar paraguayo, de Wilson Bueno*, doctoral thesis, São Paulo State University, Brazil, 2016.)

summer, tiegui, paraîpîeté, when I dropped him comme ça, with almost loving tenderness, it wasn't my silence, only my silence, without, oui oui oui my silence, which was hard, because I loved him, the oldguy, with badly discerned willingness, but I loved him, in that pure death-rattle of his ante-coma that nearly wilts the fleur, old cuñá, once so firm, of my breasts, and that cloisters me not always with locks or bars, though it could seem that way, and I felt myself decomposing in his rythme fragile, no, I only laid him sur le divan and when I went to cover his face, he'd already finished dying. Cardiac arrest said the doctor whom I called on le téléphone, with urgency and fear exagerés, añaretã, añaretãmguá, with much fear, I confide in you, you, inventive readers, more inventivist than any invention of my soul emprisonnée by these overflowings, these exaggerations of tangos and guarânias painfully arpeggiated in perfect solitude at the shore of lakes or in the deepest montagnes, in you, who decipher these words in another dimension, je confesse: there's one doubt, one great doute, morangú, that pursues me around the house and, as I've already explained, drags me into hell every time, those moments that existent, añaretã, añaretãmguá, the more than intimate doubt that somebody had killed him, the oldguy, no not a stroke or even cancer, cancer doesn't kill so quickly, the doubt lies in a deep certainty that someone, somebody—soul or snake—it doesn't matter, but it was someone and not just health, which from the recent solicitations of Dr. Paiva, I, I knew only that it was pretty good for a man of eighty-five who looked fifteen years older what with chasing after women, drink and cabaret torch songs, smoke, la fumée, anorexia, ouii, readers of my heart, somebody was the author—actor—of the death of the oldguy, that wreck whom I shouldered with sacrifice et blind ferocité. Who says I killed him? And that's where hell starts, and doesn't start, añaretã, the añaretãmguá stuff I'm talking about more than I'm talking about the oldguy, much more, and way much moreso. The oldguy was a wreck who left my life burdened and fed up. Oh, believeyoume, fed up.

Yes, I'm talking about hell, which always seems to suck until it mutinies, with invincible insensibilité, it smashes les barres of its jail and bursts out the porte, seigneur of martyrs and droughts, of the great tempêtes of locusts, tucú, locusts more biblical than all the Judeas of the world, tucú, this world I describe, morangú, the borders of death, et l'enfer, añaretã, hell, that can hide in a pair of green eyes, hovĩ, mboihovĩ, that devour you in the kitchen, just like stars on the télé, impossible yet concretely présente and with whom we so often make love, eyes shut, solitary in the bathtub of the bathroom ou, alors, as this infernal enfer de hell, añaretã, añaretãmeguá, my enfer is to possess all the stars et étoiles and every planet of the absolute cosmos and above all its chalk-grey moon, right in those green eyes so far from me that remind me of the chanson, green eyes are traitors, les yeux bleus jaloux, brown eyes loyal.

Hell is as concrèt as a stone in the sun: for the Guaratuba boy, I derailed a whole network of trains, I wept nights et days, hid my grief under the oreiller of the oldguy, so when he lay down, him, the oldster, in a sort of coma—there was no more to be done. For him I laid my trembling body in the bed, so sincerely ill, tasî, tasî tapiá, that a tiny bit more and tasî, tasî tapiá, I'd survive death, ancient dame of my pits of existence close to hell, always rolling, añaretã, rolling in my head like a sin dark and dirty with sa propre innocence.

My fear of living hasn't just to do with solitude. There's my hands and all their infinite capacités make possible, their fervor de murder ou mourir, their blazing furor at the brink of death and its waters, îtacupupú, chiã chiã, tiní, chiní, its pluie d'agonie pure, parapluie, sea of pleas and murmurs, chororó, chororó, pará-mer of drowned désirs sans limite or border, the chalk of the earth, the bad blood of everyday, ĩguasu, ĩpaguasú, oh the bad blood of everyday, tuguĩvaĩ, right down to the flies, mberú, mberú, mberú, mberuñaró, the flies and beetles of summer, laying eggs of the most pallid whiteness. Like dawn in the sea? Pará, paraná, panamá. Paraĩpĩeté.

It was from the window that I caught sight of that boy and undressed him of his flowery bermudas, he who appeared on the street in front of me, his hard thighs, his stallion knees in the sun, his seventeen years that toyed with me, pitiless, in this world of affliction with its gnawings of rare insecurité. Non, I don't wait at the window like those neighbor harpies with bad blood pressure and already old, staring at him, at him, the whole time it takes for him to walk by, down this street of straw hats and flamboyant men inflamed by rutting. Moi shut in this room, even then, I saw that he'd turned down my street, without seeing me, without goading me to devour him, me the dame of douleurs, covered in rouge et lipstick.

Beauté can be such terror![4] Añaretã-añaretãmeguá. So much monstrosité et fascination sinistre in a garçon-boy with muscular stallion thighs, at 10 o'clock on a mid-summer Thursday, just across the rue, throb throb pi'ambereté, oh pi'á, coeur et low belly, tĩegui, tĩegui, à côté instilling his convulsions, tuguĩvaí, right there where the neighbor harpies—mostly at sunset—usually see rien sauf each other moping their lives away, before the soap opera as usual, on the window-ledge while the bathers,

---

4   Refers to Rainer Maria Rilke's *Duino Elegies*.

with their plump spouses and jumpy children, full of sand, caressed by sea and caramel-dipped creamsicles, traipse nonchalantly down the road. Tecové, tecové—my eyes dart back et forth.

I simply know, more than a little, that he was un animal parfait, with smooth dark hair, and oh mon Dieu, if I saw right and nothing makes me question my certainty, the boy had two cobra-green eyes, mboihovĩ, a green so incredibly intense that at the smallest flash, a single insistent spark, they seemed to me to be the very abyss of the sea, paraĩpĩeté, vertices, verts, green, and thus hovĩ of an unnecessary savagery. I moved closer to the window and held the curtain open in studied nonchalance, so I could see him better and fully, totally in his bronzed nudité porãité, porãitereí, and above all he could see me lui watching. Pain et shadow and desire spun vertiginously on top of what was ripening in the depth of those irises that want to obliterate me. What to do? Glasses won't help, they're only good for dealing out the cards, telling fortunes, as for him, porãitereí I invent him. So with him, thigh and flesh, I only sensed the coarse freshness of his laughing face, yes, to me it was totally laughing—astounded—or atomized? I turned, though how I don't know, I must have showed him my visage étonné. Ah, taĩhu, mboraĩhu. Porenó in his arms, porenó, porenó, mongetá.

The oldguy was so concrèt and si bon, the oldguy, that I don't know, I really don't know if it was my own hands murdered him, or if it was life itself struck him dead, suddenly slugged him in his fragile heart, sweet heart, sweet, sweet, oh itty-bitty oldguy, si morose, pi'á, pi'á, I'm no cuñambatará, forgive us, littleoldone, forgive us our human failings, how insensitive. All I did, I've already said in secret, and in public too, all I did in some fit of anger, was quiet him, I repeat and insist— with much repressed amour, all I did in a fit of anger was throw him sur le sofa, he who didn't want to get out of bed, posthumous in Guaratuba, as if here, morangú, there were no sea, its beaches punctuated with umbrellas speared in the sand just like bulls speared in an arena and with flesh splayed like hunks of meat dangling on butcher hooks, tuguĩvaí, tuguĩvaí. The oldguy didn't like the sun and his skin was proof as with the least inattention, it'd come up in blisters and he'd spend three nights on fire, in agonizing douleur that analgesics could not relieve. Tasĩ, tasĩ, so miserable. Oh, my life, tecové, tinĩ. The ruin of stuff est quelque chose de frightening! May God take me before the last sticks of my precarious construction start to hit the ground. No I don't want to see myself crumbling to dust and osossoporeuses bones.

Añaretã. My current age, which I hide with shame and fear, is already quite enough and makes everything seem vain and moribund, clearly I'm talking encore une fois, añaretã, I'm speaking what I've already said, sir, sirs, ladies, readers, roses, rosebowers, clearly I am, once again, referring to hell, l'enfer. And I know that tomorrow there'll be scarcely a fleeting memory left, who knows, of the erotic memory of the boy, this young garçon with his fuzz and splendor, who right now stares up at me with that curiosity of males unbuttoned, flower of buttock and mamelon, porãitereí, porã porã, and the juice of his shoulders, of his spear, porenó, porenó, taĩhu chororó, the jus of his ardent saliva, tasting of chewing gum or menthol drops and the taste, above all, of salt in his starry eyes, hovĩ-hovĩ, mboihovĩ, gazing at me with the clameur that sex awakens in such animaux, sleeping volcan about to exploser, that will explode, cuñambatará, oh in the proferred rose of my obsession, rose of my rose, mes entre-jambes between-my-legs, oh bon Dieu, I accede to it.

Yes, hell, añaretã, añaretãmeguá, exists and, I believe, if I'm honest, that hell in my case, above all, is the desire for ever more and always more love—an unsettling insatiability that strips me completely weeping in the widowed double bed, so wide, weeping the certainty that sans doute one day, un jour, we all will die: tecové, tecové, tecovepavaerã.

So it is that I ask every strumpeter or saltpetre, where can a person descend to la caverne, in these tapevaí lands of sand in the beach town of Guaratuba? The wind, chororó, chororó, meanwhile mutes clear answers, chororó, chororó. But dans les arbres the living brute finds no peace, tecové, the living brute of my marafona floozy body, captive, craved. What kind of act—sepulchre or song—is dying? Morangú, morangú: but before death shows up, and it'll be tomorrow morning, I'll sing behind my crystal ball, to the golden tinkle of my bracelets, I'll recount, to the first parishioner, a fable, morangú morangú, a fable of love, I'll recount it, and may it be sublime.

Autumn panic frequently draws near to the mysterious peripheries of death. Thus autumn is hell. Añaretã. Añaretãmeguá. That's what I feel, as if it were an embrace closing in to haunt me, the sole embrace suffered in my life of errors and conveniences. Everyone's giggling in Guaratuba: I secretly hide in the autumn attics of the beach town. Men, women, newborn babes, babes about to be born, babes who were once born, the automne panique of their raspy voices, the panic at having balanced, all this time, on the taut precipitous tightrope of those acrobats who won't let themselves be carried off by mediocrity. Caught in the midst of the uncommon. As for all those teeming folk, they're totally ordinary and bureaucrats to boot, all touched by the machine, the State, the fetid powers that be. As for me, I'm inscribed in the heart of the marginal, of those cast aside and crestfallen in diners dogged by all that is vain and barren. Jaguara. Jaguará. Jaguaraíva. Jaguapitã. Death's thus not so definitive: moral glass-fragile mortal. Non, I can't get used to the fact that my panique starts right where their vacationing lives begin. Vacation from what??, if it's mixed with words and slaps and the one who pushes down the suitcase lid realizes they've hit bottom. Oh, it's terrible, it's as terrible as a thing inflamed, the incroyable flight of the flesh and fur of night bats scribbled dans le noir with moonlight, andirá andirá andiráimevá.

Fright is one thing, but panic, oh there's nothing quite like panique. Et la chose la plus curieuse is that panic doesn't existe. In my view it's an invention from the depths of our heads touched as they are by martyrdoms and circumlocutions of the abyss. Some cases perish like le wind, they don't exist but it's as if they existent. Distinct from a tree, from a birrd, distinct from the sea although the sea holds other deeper and even more extensive mayhem. Fright is entirely a quick sketch of panic, this dust in dust in poussière poussée that doesn't exist but it's as if it exists, and when it vanishes, it's as if it never jamais happened. Pure enchantment, enchained.

Enchanting enchantery. What other image could there be for human action? Fright's the acute spectre de panique, a thing that is its intimate ghost, something close to the pre-pre-riskiness, the before of the befores of the before. The ancestors and the elders.

I write so that my heartstrings don't snap dedans: I write night et jour, hounded, harassed, here in the wind of the beach resort dans le triste rythme of these winter days: weather swirling and the humid shadows of sombreros, of step and spits in the landscape of the paths all pocked with sand and salt. Gutters drip onto the cladding of the house. Humidity lingers there where mildew starts to weave its secret life. And, so that those inner spaces where death saunters nonplussed like tarantulas won't arise, I write this down, squandered and lugubrious. I, the unhinged marafona floozy of the beach town, glued to the vieillard— his most enchanting hourglass, sponge gripped to the spilled remains of the wreck. When his blood stops, I too will probablement go extinct. The oldguy's emaciated thigh annonces his crashing end, for tomorrow, but each new jour, the stubborn existence du vieillard puts paid to the possibilité that he could be face à face with death. And if he doesn't die, it seems nous aussi we're guaranteed a bit more, clawed out with nails and screeches, of this scarce élément they call la vie. Life—

caustique and feral. Some days unruly tango, and others, a shuffling cha-cha-cha.

I desire only that my deepest nature stay plopped on this sofa, at three in the afternoon of this wintery hemispheric beach town. I forget the tough Afro-brasilien floozies, Guaraní and Castilian, parce que I know I'm writing and writing is like taking all that surrounds a living body and scribbling it on the walls of Main Street. No need to hold anything back of silence—these communicating vessels, the rouge des veines, the kick in the guts, voices et voix, beats and barks—everything can be told and vividly set down. And—because—all my mots, my words set loose in the setting wind—will be fewer, irrevocably fewer than those martyred adverbs inscribed as History. I'm my own construction et ainsi je me considère the first to blame for all the fallen scaffolding of my attempted projet. Will I find myself? Je ne sais pas et I persevere, as best I can: writing my story down even if it gives me shooting douleurs in my ovaries et un saut in the pulse of a vein near my heart.

And now I'd like to tell you just one big hairy secret: all my energy goes into pulling myself up by the bootstraps and into the immense armies of ants, all those sounds silencieux murmured by ants, the harmless insectes that are Guaraní as it rises in me, ant-

like, tahiĩ, tahiĩguaicurú, araririi, aracutí, pucú. Ants of
divinity blazing up in this dusk of verbs and nouns, in
ıy tangle-web webtangle—capable in me, blessed lady,
' deciding, with sudden verdict, my fate here among
you antediluvian beings. Oui, because I'm born each
ıatty moment of the moment du moment raté. Et I will
be until the end of le possible. And then I'll head off
there when there's no more ici. Añaretã is hell and we
finally realize its flames exert their power only in the past
et le futur—they don't enter or feel the présent, añaretã,
they don't go there or account for it, the simple fact is
that the présent is the home of the almighty Deity whose
job it is to deal avec the dead or heap whatever tasks it
likes upon the living. In the past, in Asunción, Birigüi,
Poconé, Campo Grande, no matter, the Imposed Thing
precipitated itself with diamond-hard eyes and the futur
seems to spear—grinning, trident, lewd lord of plague,
horror and acrity—all lavisciousness and débaucherie,
that existent only to plant afflictions, cacti, and fright
in the présent tense. But I rip its inhospitable flesh out
of the now and eat it whole so that the world returns to
me as honey. No, Guaraní is harmless and I fork it up,
nibbled by tahiĩ tahiĩguaicurú, sylphs, aracutí, araririi,
pucú. Winged ants that pick the song from my mouth
so as to penetrate me, insistent, with their wings, the
wedding dance de l'abyss, their whirr at the back of the

nasal cavité, their piercing death-agony, ah, the words de
Guaraní they soothe my bones: tahiĩguaicurú, araririĩ,
aracati, pucú, pucú.

like a game of make-believe: pimpimbaristas, slenderpretty flower, doe-crazy, Sinsinhatty, thwhistle, cinderbella, honeysucker, fireflyes, basting antennae, housemarvel, complutely crazies, bumballs, silksilly, yellowbellies, hideinseek, zinzibabwes, walkabyllies, wheels o'fortune whistles, teresa bejeeza, cowgirl tracings, cute blindsdown, catatonicks, consternators, frillysillies, roseygoos, dark mystère of fabulous origin, trances, troupes, helicopterous silligigs, cancans, glass cabinetes, duendes, vagueries, consenting abdominals, bronchious sylphs, festivating lumpens, perennial lumpens, tout comme un jeu of make-believe: the vieux guy contemplative but his hard world yessirreebob, a deadly force, yes, primed to exist in the pouvoir of thigh or in the blood vomité by machineguns, sentiers, rebounded luggers, the face of care, la face de cake, the face of break and breakdown, dead eyes derrière guerrilla handkerchiefs, spongey nymphos, in the end you couldn't keep it going, this story, its inner legends, its slant of branch, its anarquick lenses, its irremediable tenderness, potencies, prados, adelias[5], its trod of vomissement, this story wishes et désires only to be a game of rope-a-dope: like the gods in the beginning, in the tupã-karai, before the début de tout et all, les dieux and their coup de dés, their macabre inventurings, oguera-jera, this world achy: like a round of rope-a-dope: ñe'ẽ.

Remember, life, do you remember: our maison in Asunción, rivulets of water, Guaraní country, and le oldguy, pas aussi old as now, though gaunt and mostly because of that, it's instinct that propels his satyr life and needs. He sought me out, after that cinquième glass of wine, the fifth, suddenly, gaunt et faking insouciance, starting to grope me with tickles, and knowing I wouldn't go for it, I burst into a run, I'm onto the oldguy's game and I dash out of the room. His fun and martyrdom: chasing me, hunting me, haunting me. Reaching me, inevitably as usual, he wrestled me to the ground (just as I later had to throw him on the sofa), smooth varnish where I flailed, butterfly souffrante, while he mounted the hard bones of his knees on my quavering arms, clothes défaits, all his vêtements, the first rasps of his skin on my peau, his snouty thumb and sexe en flamme touching me in all that I offered him. He stuck his bouche béante

---

5   Refers to Brazilian poet Adélia Prado (1935–   ).

on me as if to suck me totalmente into his hot insides. Yes, aortan blood pulsed in every pore of the oldster. Even though I'd, once certain caprices were satisfied, for magasins et jewels, cadeaux and grabbags, spit back all that his avid tongue had proferred me in his salive with its undecipherable goût of semen. He tripudiated and wasn't yet that wreck whom I always expected to die, who dies and doesn't die and about whom, for the nth time je déclare formellement et atteste: it weren't moi qui killéd the oldie.

Raining. Winter wet pluies of southern hemispheric June in the beach town. Dense fog, thick, a sort of paste of days when the rains start to soak even gardens and streets. An evocation of fairies through the windows: all marrying winter, leurs sombreros s'embracent in an orgy of wet leaves. I swear. Raining right to the bones of his bloodless face, the empty hollow là there where his profil emerged dans l'ombre, emaciated sketch of what his face once exuberantly was, déjà old, but still concrète as stone and not what it finalement became. I swear. Afflicted only by the unrelenting souffle that suffocated him, freed him from the bedsheets, from his tight collar, and I lugged him from bed to sofa, afflicted and a little hysterical and—why not say it—with a pinprick of dark hatred for his vegetative and estranged persistence.

His smile of gratitude et fondness, his eyes still spoke en furie, his sourire I can't prove because a smile's subjective and particular, but I can say, with brute honesty, he was still alive. Then, and this is already in another temps, returning to suffocate him with a pad, given he was blubbering in a diarrheic désir to return to the bed, I just had him contained there on the sofa when I realized that, sans avis ni raison, the oldie already turned into a new masque of the oldie, now more contained and even though his teensy weensy eyes blue with cataracts stared bulging at the toit (or at my tits?), for the première fois I saw a certain flash of decency dans la face of that vieux bastard qui a ruiné my life. Non, it wasn't out of the bleu that I pulled him from bed to sofa, but to keep him still, though my hands trembled in that démence that must précède human murder—be it scorpion-suicide, be it the venom-wave of the wind. All I did was move him from one spot to un autre, and as such, the task of dying, properly speaking, was la exclusive responsabilité of the oldie. I can trumpet it avec ma bouche wide open, even if no one gives a shit: it wasn't moi who killéd le vieux guy.

Sometimes the only thing that settles me is the bed that was ours, mine and the oldster's, before his—fateful—move onto the sofa, an old carved walnut four-poster bed with the holy image of Our Lady I'd hung on the headboard, I sit here on the bed as if everything were poised to crumble and with the harsh shock of being unable to withstand this irrepressible desire to weep, desire that starts in a nostalgic dream, all yesterday and music and resplandeur and all that's wasted on Princes Uncharming—pasodoble, torero, espagnol. No, I realize, nothing ever came easy to me, nothing warned me of the cards dealt by the oldie and his inevitable fin. Pas de scintillation apart from this painting here of scream et panique et studied errors. Life itself, that terrain of urgencies and heartburn, Dieu has taken from me, taken away, above all, his silvery jus, here where ça pulse, that symptom stronger than malaise which some call by the strange nom de happiness. Je ne sais pas if in this life there's really happiness, that abysmal sentiment of bonheur forged from the terreur of ecstasy, renunciation, assumptions and the choral chanson by which the gardenia imposes such a savage and disquieting air in the garden.

It's all disputable amidst the bustle of the boy and his posturing, as if this were a happiness, I'm not convinced, mainly after he vanishes, crossing the first street corner, all I see is his shoulder-blade and bum, his torso, his mane of splendid black curls and who knows if la vie is all just a big guffaw, the frank flow of a heart gone to pasture, now out for lonely drinks, toute seule, verres de wine, they warm my stomach and even, a bit, my frigid soul. It's that every time he goes past, the boy, it's like he's never coming back and not that I'm deliriously needy and triste, an insatiable nymphomaniaque, no, the rawest vérité is that the boy affirms and swears and trembles, peremptory, that he's never going to ever return again because I, and here I read between the lines, provoke in him an absolute rejection of all disgust and fear.

In the bedroom with the oldie—who doesn't notice a thing at this point—je smear my whole face with rouge and lipstick. I stay hours and heures devant le miroir, smearing, coloring, with earrings and baubles, the raffia wig, the scandalous mouth, while I hesitate between buying and not buying new perfume for there's no guarantee that the oldie's sense of smell has diminished. The eau de toilette, the parfums, the Paraguayan colognes, all of them, the more the oldster caught a whiff of them, the more promiscuous he became and devoted to sex, the oldguy's sexe, old yes but not as old as today, yes today, yes, when it's already no longer possible. So I make do with stale déodorisant Coty and the oldguy keeps on sleeping, mouth open and snoring through his nose, forgotten by everything of this here-and-now drowning in sponges, colors, carmines. The masque of my pouffiasse floozy face, this marafona face I see in the miroir, is a face something close to those cubist paintings or of the radical abstractionists—the living stain of a visage that sees itself and still doesn't understand a thing. If the boy were to catch me like this in this get-up and maquillage, he'd run off breathless as if he'd seen a panicked scarecrow. And the oldie, were he to see again, would spit his choleric baba of impotent revenge in my face. Those same eyes that despite the smile had stared rudely at me, right in the eye, iris to iris, point fléché à point fléché, as with effort and irritation I dragged him from the wide bed to le sofa where I could settle him, if he weren't already dead, seated perfectly.

Suruvu is the word-soul turned birrd: such flights, my cardinals, the watery chirp of the suruvu in solitude, because imprisoned in the harsh organism of an entity written alive in the ayvu, sweet agonies, martyred in the tremulous throat of those all too human—word-bird transmuted into soul, suruvu and its morning roar each dawn in the face of the day to come, sea and fig tree, suruvu is much of what I speak and un peu plus than what things speak as they pass through me, through Brinks, through the oldie and above all through the boy—that burrowing and flaming flash that brought me face to face with fate, since the oldie was dying, and I, and I needed to live, even if he whacked death in the nuts and in his own ailing body found the terminal solution. If this is true, I secretly conclude that the oldguy killed himself in me and, I pray, it wasn't me who killéd him, lui, the oldie.

: i'm through with the purchase of cloths, diapers, gases and injections, that took me on breathless visits to the pharmacy, one dusk après une autre I sit ici on this sofa diagonal to the window, and once seated it's presque as if I were totally crumbling: cramps in the guts: setting sun weaving humid nuances: spaces from où move déjà les occupations cérémoniales of light and lune: between the shady crowns or entre les durs voids of the fig trees that devastate the crépuscule of the beach town with shadow et suspicion; figuier, couronne, shade: la ancestral speech of pères et grands-pères that infinitely vanishes into memory, they entertain all speech et tricot: those Guaraní voices turn tender only if they persist in weaving: ñandu: there is no better fabric than the spiderweb of the leaves tissées together: figuier: shade: their woven leaves in unison, ñándu, in unison et between the arabesques that, symphoniques, interweave, chess of green and bird et chanson, in the happy amble of a freedom: ñandutí: ñandurenimbó:
: here I sit: ñandutí: weaving into the crochèterie my ñandutí lace: ñandutimichĩ: smallest ti-fleur that my

needle pursues with excruciating patience for hours and hours: in this hand-stitching, salt-clocks slowly tick off the fluctuating couleurs du coucher du soleil that sets in les automnes of now: here ñandutí: opacité of feeling: je m'assois: je m'sens: ñandutí: being a Cancer my verb is sentir: to sense or feel: me voir: ñandutí: winter more than automne panique automne: ñandutí: what is the secret d'identité entre these deux things absolument distinctes: spiders and scorpions?

: yes, scorpions of the heart: ñandutí: they alight and sting you, pincent you with all they've got: the ñandutí jolt mortally occurring: meanwhile we survive: even if ostrich-necked, ñanduguasú: stuck in sand: ñandu: ñandutí: spiderweb: the crochet stitches contorting from one to the next: corolla: ramification of hair and ligne: slowly announcing the fleur of flower most florid: most michĩ: ñandutimichĩ: almost invisible: miraculum: simulacrum: ñandutí: mirroir of the gods: ñandutí: a thousand at times solitaire ñandutí: the needle as dark désir for blood et death: the oldie each second ticking older: the boy: how can they be so green, hovĩ mboihovĩ: eyes of the boy with their myriad green flecks that give them color: hovĩ hovĩ hovĩ: my despair bigger than the cicada-loud nuit of the beach town of Guaratuba où I hear myself die: marafona floozy: only a passenger on this sea: la mer: paraná: ñandutí made from a shuttle chasing a further lacing: the ever repeated gesture of conducting the thread from the linearity of the skein that hops at our feet in a rumble of thread set free:

: soon the oldie will grunt: the ferocious bite of the cobra will not be as frightening et obscur et presque mortal as are those paniques of the oldie: he bets against death or fumes at uberlife: ñandu: ñandutimichĩ: laaaaacings crocheted: faster than a single heartbeat: race of fingers and filaments and us: ñandutí: spiderweb almost evaporable: ñandurenimbó: just as the thread threads and threads through these modest dusks never arriving at their profond coeur: ñandutí: so light are your ties and knots and all and tout: the grunts of the oldguy: where do they go after he emits them, those errors of the oldie?: lighter than air and mountain: ñandutí:

: my helpless abandonment would be moins or less if it weren't for all these longues silences pendant these hours, diagonal à l'abyss: the flowering octahedron of immortal consistency: the chase: consistency: the living knot: microscopic accentuation with which all and anything can get mixed up in a single and mécanique push of the needle: fatal: i stick it in and keep sticking it: like whoever stabs justice even if it's slow: a stitch of finest crochet: ñandu: ñandutí: ñandurenimbó: a single solitary stitch to the web almost beyond ocular or human comprehension: ñandu: mobile stitches: minimal millions will escape from their eggs on the fragile ligne of this web: ñandurenimbó: millions fleeing: hetaicoé: beaucoup de many millions: ñandumichĩ: ñandutí: in the hunt for life: now: hetaicoé: having to tear themselves free until they are fully spiders: their pattes: these hairy and horrible things that slowly move across la table and can enter the sleeve of your shirt: ñanducavayú: no one is capable of staunching their honorable venom: now millions escape the eggs to populate patio and kitchen starting tomorrow morning: and even with these many and millions I'm still alone: after all spiders are just spiders: ñandu: ñandutí:

: shadows pass subtly through the apartment full of light: the mosaic of bricks that made the oldie, before he was so old, happy: bare feet stepping, stepping all over what I'd worked to sweep and dust clean: back then the shards of glass, on my most hysterical day, should never have been removed: they'd have cut the oldguy's Achilles heel and a seule veine that in hemorrhaging would have made him faint: an absolument empty being from whom all essence had been withdrawn: the shadows sketch figures of memory: they fray once the spiderweb is done: ñandu: ñandutí: web ñandutí: another thread and what can't be seen enters fully into me: frayed sunset lights: new autumns of our woes: the dark inheritance of the gods: the oldster: lourd fardeau: so lightweight: frayed: brick et shadow: a lacy mosaic: world facing a new knot: the launching: unexpected sting that pricks us before we realize: añaretã: hell: what I desire: non, oh lord: what je désire is simple: ñandutí: miniscule flowerbloom made out of our riches new craftings: ñandutí: ñandurenimbó:

: the oldguy, with every afternoon that passes, is closer to death: gases: injections: pills of various colors: the oldguy is closer, I repeat, to dying: I don't want to get up from the sofa diagonal to the sky of the window: I'm sitting here: my hair almost hides the efforts of my crochet: teenytiny harpoon in the needle's tip: knot: twist: loop: loop: knot: twist: the weave growing: useless: still a nothing: without form to make it into a brassière or song: he can weep, he can suffer: non, I refuse to see it!,[6] the oldie's spilled blood, ¡que no quiero verla!: bra or song: the crocheting has barely begun: I don't know how he's going to die: from what depth the final moment will come to demolish him; ñandu: if in a chokehold the afternoon were to confiscate his air: or if it'd be but a sigh: he'd stay pressed into the abyss: aortan blood interrupted: the scar of days: hemorraghic death: septicemia: or nothing but a passing fatigue of the heart: I don't know what's being woven: interwoven: interlace: loop and knot: new knots: other twists: a fabric of intrigue: maybe it's a shroud:

6 Refers to Lorca's poem "Lament for Ignacio Sanchez Mejias."

maybe undershorts: or vessel: ñandutí: to cover my plus intime sexe: none can know off the bat the spider's secret fabrications: ñandu: ñandurenimbó:

: today le boy made me hear the murmures of the lunaire storm: in the swelter of siesta, I knew suddenly and à bout de souffle that he'd come: shadow et profil: fulsome foufounes: nipples: hard thighs riding: son contour sharp: the chestnut silkfloss of his cheveux: I bite, remorse-bitten: ñandu: ñandutí: the needle nestling in: crochet: escargot: curve: the corde: araignée: spider: ñandu: le boy awakens everything in me: already my skin and hair raise their hackles in a shudder: c'est moi l'énigme and hunted hummingbird hawk-moth: I've got to devour him ever imprévisible: stroking his brazen sex in the g-string: but above all his eyes green in a face of laugh and soleil: the thorax in the ravages de vent et de lament: to danse in siesta: rêve: je suis his spider: algebra: ready-to-go boa: partout his adept tongue licks me: I anoint him totally with salive and drool: humors: sweats: the miasmes: les spasmes: the siesta sets my deep uterus ablaze: le boy: suddenly ñandu: maybe he'll just laze his tongue out and run it over me: de mes pieds jusqu'au ciel in mourning where I glimpse the murmures of the lunar storm: lip contre lip: spider and clampearl: la danse de sa bouche: ñandu: the h'arpoon of the n'eedle crosses the line weaving lineal: before nudité the wantonness of piss: ñandurenimbó: I force his tête upon my mouth: erase the baton from him: the eraser: erase the line: la siesta; my cry: never forget the sigh of the boy before all et tout were transformé: spiderweb, wet mist and clouds in the murmurs of the lunar storm: of un seul mortal sigh: mine and his: the fiery couteau of his lance: fired: point final: knotted: lancée: knot: launched: period: ñandutí: ñandu: the web loses interest: the lights se perdent in the growing nocturnal bleu: web d'araignée: spiderweb: ñandu: maybe the boy will retourne tomorrow: or it could all be encore and newly no more than the oblique projection of a marafona floozy in grief: ñandu: look there: this boy qui traipses over cobblestones sans even knowing j'uberexiste: out here in the dusk: rêve de sleep become the ruby capitulation of the being who can but see him: he who walks so imperiously: toward the mer: his taste of conch and salt: I spin and spin et tisse the web: ñandutí: lacy: renderings: imagination rendered fabrile: figue-tree heure: iguane: ñandurenimbó: à la sieste: today in these stifling tuesdays: massed mercredis: après-midi: the faun:[7] I had le boy tooth and nail: I had him couched in my belly's entrails: ñandu: spiderweb: ñandutí: only he doesn't know it: and the sea still holds

---

7 Refers to Stéphane Mallarmé's "L'après-midi d'un faune," considered by Paul Valéry to be the greatest work of French symbolist poetry. Taken up later in music by Debussy and in dance by Nijinsky.

his taste and semen: even son sexe ne peut pas câcher les trâces: evaporable veil: ñandutí: transparence et lumières: ñandu: ñandurenimbó:

Now here's le trou: the hole of the hole in le centre. No, no more do the inks of blood dribble trickling et douleureux from carpète to salon, through all the bedrooms, the living room, lingering, stalling because there's still more, on the veranda, there where he, oldie, whiled away heures, with his asthme and tachycardia and, above all, totalement shriveled in his melancholy heart already affecté by his eighty-five years. I've gotta say it, I who intensely know the pit, the cavern, that grimace en bas de la ligne de hell: le trou, le trou du hole in the center. Craters?

I'm not going to cry, not going to get all weepy and sob all snively into the pillow. But how, comment puis-je get past this? It's so disenchanting to vivre. From what height of dignité might I find the math that can show me, can show me the way? Je n'sais pas, I know only that what I see autour de moi is the slow sinking of sun into the sea, suprème wheel of fire et métal like an open sore in the regrets of heaven.

Il n'y a pas de silence more profond, more itself than the high silence of death or of les étoiles, so that the silence of his stellar absence, grabbing me by the neck, like a monstreuse forme of octopus that, slimy and repugnant, ensnares the heart—entangled there—this always unexpected suffering that loss brings us, defeat, failure contumacious with a lonely pining, the pining of *saudade* sans retour ni futur.

Here I'll reste. The house entire is sinking into high autumn nuit. One star and another are already up there, nailed into the blue, nocturnal and vesper, star, mainly star. There's little noise and in the background a whole orquestration of cicadas in heat imposes itself in a vacarme that vibrates beneath the stridence affligée, with un peu de all the stuff that courses through the world—footsteps, bikes, horns, the moteurs des speeding scooters of the guys who hang out on treeless corners during the Holy Week holiday. Little big world of the beach town of Guaratuba all energized by les souffrances of Christ. Now, for example, the sea suffers the bashing of its waves, which I can hear from here, in this house that the death of the oldie has left me—like an gratuitous triomphe. I'd say the same about our joint chequing account in the state bank—in every way, fundamental.

I remember everything. I narrate and novelize entangling tout and am so lost I don't recognize myself in cette face that time's been bulldozing—harshly and sans pitié. The hollow of the crater in the center isn't quite hell but close enough—with its decelerated and disjointed movement full of all that a sad being lacks, one as sad as I am, pitched headlong, near this ocean that, in the end, at the end of it all, I didn't choose just to let my life sink there—like a castaway bottle flung out to sea.

I'm still here, and this is the only possible world. I dream of nice houses, aristocratic dogs of the dalmatian breed loping in the meadows of a huge mansion in the States, mirages, paths that découvre delirium. Why oh why can't a person reach happiness via these rêves in technicolor? Only one thing is beyond all doubt: death. La mort. All the rest is fiction, drame, télévision, littérature.

No, I'd never wanted to imagine him in the pit of the mine, his curlicued hairs, those hairs of the boy, I mean, the prodigious offer of his whole body of flesh made golden in the sun, the sun of that melancholy Guaratuba solstice. Nor am I referring to his thigh and buttocks, nor, in this silence now, do I remember his exclusive manners and the ways of his soft caress made of juice and tremeur and anxiety and vomit, but always only mine, exclusively mine—the uncontained willingness with which, legs open, I gave myself to him. And I get him to hold my breasts in the cup of his hands, the unpardonable flaccidity that makes me a floozy today and tomorrow, they're covered in maggots, my own breasts, in wriggling maggots that make voracity and hunger last forever.

Yes, the girl: almost impossible to describe, in my tachycardiac heart, ay, he's killing me, ay I feel sick suddenly, almost impossible to describe how his mouth feels, sunk into the mouth of that mundane babe who strolls in vain on beaches, who parades her scandalous g-strings and all the vulgar rest, ay I still want him badly, mama mia, ay life is unsurmountable, almost impossible to describe for you how his skin that is my peau goes all aroused instead for that sirène sans imagination ou personnalité with her Miss Universable body and nothing else. I can't tell you how they revolt me, those disgusting nymphes. A woman really worthy of this treatment should already have a ripe seed in her or have been bitten by the living scorpion of authentic happiness, so sincere when she was younger, her happiness of uterus and drool and mucus and saliva. And of the howls of orgasme.

No, reader, don't ever go chasing after what they call appearances: a nymph-body can also burn in hell. But for him, for this boy who makes me hoot from ferocious love and wander weeping in the streets of this beach town, rebellious, eyes sunken, look at her now, the crazywoman, they cast stones for she is, more than floozy, whore, crummy soothsayer, look at that witch, the boy was my rise and fall, all the months of passion, calvaries, crosses, thorns, for the boy who set me afire with his face ardent with soleil. The brutal summer light of Guaratuba. What would it be like to be dead in the sweat and sultry heat? The oldster knew it all. But his dead heart won't tell.

What is love? A solitary rose in the desert? Ou the simple odious feeling that it is impossible, it is impossible to live in it, without falling and getting up, without getting up and falling all over again, recurrent, sombre compulsion of devotees to the harsh profession of loving without measure or limit, of those marked by this love and whom I see in the cards and who are made shadow or the spectre of the cloud that settles here over the sea of Guaratuba, in a word, intime avec the clap of thunder, the word happiness, artifice that we too cultivate so as not to suddenly stop dreaming. It'd be, surely, très sad if les gens humains were to suddenly lose the strange inclination that is both error and duty, the job of dreaming. No one can keep going without the wailings and rages and sudden scarlet jealousies of love. To you I déclare: a photonovel is far more than photo and much more than novel; a photonovel is life set down on paper, and though its follies and missed moments ache, the kisses and the inevitable final happiness don't really occur and are just drawn out on paper in the end. Stuff of the imagination.

A drink in the bar, and it passes, it's passing, I still want to marry death and am buying myself a silver-plated pistol on the sly for mes moments of panique. All I desire is the mortel silence of the étoiles in the huge skies of this beach town of Guaratuba, as night draws close and the sea begins to vanish in dark mystère. Another drink, suddenly I bawl and wander streets, cheap bars, cognacs, street corners, I keep walking, in anguish and blood, in supreme loathing because that boy isn't really mine, oh dear blessed Virginne of Guadalupe, without his face, his body, his sexe and the skin of his hands, without them I'll never manage to live, me who lives from fortune, only Dieu knows what terreur comes with a glimpse of le futur, it makes a person founder, without recourse or rémède, at the pit of the pit of the cave of hell. No one tries to understand, reader most dear, no one dares to comprehend what is already set down with blood, iron and fire in the seeping wounds of le destin.

Look he's crossing the street on his bike in the colors of the rainbow. My God, his skin burnt by summer, his infant et adolescent skin, the exact curve of buttocks and his unnameable victoire d'exister, look at how he looks at me with his green gaze, that boy for whom I dragged myself onward without feeling that I lived among earthly men, I dragged myself through the avenues and street corners of Guaratuba, the vast sea right in front of me, as if it were the last hope of a life that really wanted itself dead, eaten by fish-slime and algae and formaldehyde.

By the window, I felt, as fact ou tragédie, that he, that he was already mine—from before the Déluge, even from before any of this was written down, his crisp and vegetal gaze, the muscle of his arms and—what I could not foresee or freiner—the devestating conflagration that his nascent existence has provoked in me in these years I'm living, doubled, bitter aftertaste in the ash, I mean to say, in the saliva, the cape, the cape-of-good-hope.

Psychic stargazer that I am, trollop et floozy of Guaratuba, only I know how much the longing hurts and how it hit me when, pretending isolation, I flopped on the windowsill, watching the movements of late afternoon, gens, sparrows, rufous-collared sparrows, and he passed by me like one who arrives for a decisive kidnapping, without turning back or possibility of flight.

And he remained—for all time—made an entité or serpentité.

At first, before I even said he was coming, even before I knew his nom, age or surname, he enteréd the house, in his flowery bermudas, yellow chemise tied at his waist, his young bronco waist, and took me over, first with his hands, then with his mouth and so on successively until there we were, naked and unashamed, eating each other up with féline and disparate voracité, with mother and fils hunger.

Later, much later, he shut his eyes and lay his head of gold in my lap, me sitting up in bed, he let himself doze off. It was only then that I perceived: there was in him an urgency et his affection was the scarcely unleashed désir of animals that commence to live. I, more ingenuous than his seventeen years, assumed that such a face was the face of what is conventionally called love.

The oldster, who'd die at seven in the evening in a hemispheric wintry June, still prowled the house and I could hear, with a frightening clarité, his coughs, his sputums et ses sarcasmes, the oldguy, that wreck so harshly loving that he filled my life and made me a dame-of-fortune out of pure caprice, because the oldie ensured there was nothing I lacked, not even simple nail polish or pail of sassafras.

I didn't want, in all sincerité, didn't want anything to do with even the odeur of the oldguy impregnating the bedroom or with the bitter wafts so characteristique of médicines or with the heavy atmosphère of this sickroom where in summer the boy of Guaratuba planted a sun of incredibly natural incandescence. Let the oldguy die, die and stay dead as a doornail, that wreck I hoisted with the mind of someone qui transportes a man already dead toward death, him and his eighty-five years and all the extra ones he devoured, with rancour and bad luck, in the sickness acquise in the cabarets of Aquidauana.

That's why I give you the gift of the Angel. It's so cruel and petty de moi to do this, like someone who looks you in la face all innocent and caring, and who with extrème caution, pulls out from beneath her dress hem, without you noticing, the supreme terror of three scorpions that enact a life et death struggle in her lap. This is it, this is what it is, this gift I give you, to you who read me dear reader as if you were discreetly pressed to the crack of a shut door.

Brinks: it's only for you my panting heart gives a shudder, only for you and your wiggly and teenytiny tail, loopy and always happy. Brinks'i. At this moment when the treetops weave their winter in the beach town of Guaratuba, and all goes frigide under the roofs, above all the oldguy who in winter is dying and à cause de ça spills the wine and sinks into trembling, trembling, as if spilling death in a single gulp and goal—lethal. At such moments, I wake up with lugubrious lyrics of remorse gripping my left side, the rotten poison of the pining of *saudade,* and my entire body is clenched in the desire to kill or die. Perhaps, perhaps, perhaps.[8] Chororó, guarará, chororó.

Brinks'imi: yes, yes, it's you I talk to, plaything of fur lying leashed in my lap, so cuddly, as if born exclusively for this life, wee tongue lolling skilfully, you're so floozerific at times, eh, Brinks, whatcha saying, whatdya say? A Paraguayan girl always delivers, as in the letters that, now, for a long time, I've forgotten what it feels like to receive. No one writes to the floozy[9]. Brinks'i. Brinks'imi.

Oh, Brinks'michĩ, Brinks'michĩ, it's so cold on this beach where you walk with me, simple friend, witness of all these years already, and you're getting on in years, though old just refers to one person, him, hey, Brinks? Right, Brinks'i? Right, Brinks'michĩ?, wee teenytiny pup et cutesy, teenytiny pointy nose, glass-button eyesies, my bitsywitsy beingski who wriggles, oh, how he wriggles in the sand of this humide street. Calisse, Brinks!, if tu keep dashing and tangling me up, ici et là, underfoot, ah, Brinks'i, if you keep winding around my legs, I'll trip on your leash and land flat on the ground. And if I bust a bone? And if they're full of osteoporoporoses? But your

---

8 "Quizás, Quizás, Quizás" (known in English as "Perhaps, Perhaps, Perhaps"), is a popular bolero song by Cuban songwriter Osvaldo Farrés, a 1947 hit later covered in English by Desi Arnaz, Nat King Cole, Doris Day, among others. The 1992 Australian film *Strictly Ballroom* featured the 1964 Doris Day version.

9 This refers to García Márquez, *El coronel no tiene quien le escriba* (*No One Writes to the Colonel*).

bustle, for a chien of almost seventeen (more long-lived than tortoises or dinosaurs), ah Brinks'i, it's amazing, it's only this that makes me burst again into gales of laughter at life.

Non: I've got Brinks, my Brinks'i, Brinks'imi, Brinks'michĩ. Oh, I'm not going to tell you, adoring and maternal toy of my floozy life, anything, my precious, about how cold it is in the beach town of Guaratuba in the winter fog, with the sea like verre clouded by the pluies and rain. Brinks'i, Brinks'michĩ.

There's no more boy, only the oldguy persists with his amputated prick that still keeps itching, only that calisse d'oldie whom I lug on my back, holding me fast in his camp de concentration, Brinks! And I already forget you've been alive like this for seventeen willful years, I've already forgotten everything, j'oublie and start to bawl.

The same corner dépanneur across the street, Brinks'i, its façade and the pallid madame qui me vend a glass of cognac, disgust in her glinty viper eyes—the fear or even admiration I provoque in the natives of this exiled crumbling bit of seaside in Guaratuba of the province of Paraná, chaque fois that I step outside—am I witch or guru?

No one gets that in this doggone world of merde or shite, it's just unending agonie that makes me want to see him again, the boy, him in the rusty and lonely game of foosball, where he strutted, in feline and singular agility, his bare chest like a fixed flag of majestic beauty, la lune tattooed on the right side de son thorax, the lumière of his green eyes in the middle of le bar, mboihovĩ, hovĩ, hovĩ, him, madame, it's him, you puritan pouffiasse with no connection to Guaratuba, it's him I'm talking about and I remember, yes, him, don't answer me you daughter-of-a-dagnabbed-bitch!, don't answer me, I am fate and fortune, yes, I am, oui, I also am she who jiggles 17 year olds, minors, madame! It's me, it's me, the marafona floozy of Guaratuba.

Forgive me, Brinks, for these heartfelt exclamatory somnambulisms. Oui, Brinks'i, Brinks'-michĩ, no one can do or dream anything good for someone like me, right now, I realize all exits are shut. Brinks'michĩ. Brinks'michĩmi. Me and you walking, just the two of us, side by side, who is more imprisoned now by gut feelings? Who's older than the tortoise now?

Oh, Brinks'i, me and you strolling down the little alley to the beach at the end of Prosdócimo Street. No, there's no use in me spitting on the pauvre madame who runs the bar, no use in me trying to trick her or scratch her face with my trollop jaguar nails on her skin. There's one solution: leave, and head wherever the wind will carry us.

What filthy sand you're playing on, where you sonorously piss in childish happiness and full of laughter! Brinks'michĭ. Brinks'michĭmi.

But I, who am I? I'm still muddled, by cognac and life, by my pining for the boy of summer given over to me like a fetus yanked alive into the human profession. Only you understand me, only you, my teenytiny Brinks, tender eyesies dark like jaboticaba, earlets alert to silence, wee wagging tail. Brinks'michĭmíra'ymi.

Brinks'michĭmíra'ymi, you make me so happy, oh flagile innocence, emitting a few wimpy yips in the fishmarket, Brinks, frail and teenytiny as you are, Brinks'michĭmíra'ymi, what a Bulldog, wee saucer of milk where wet biscuits are dissolving, constantly, you know, and special treats, Brinks, my companion, in clamors and mornings. Brinks'michĭmíra'ymi.

How can anyone keep living in these clots of sand and salt, Brinks, your sugar sweetness, the afternoon's soon over and the fog of wintry south-hémisphèric June is utterly grey, the sun opaque, lustrous as furniture, there in our house, oh I know, in our house begin the ashes that flood the heart, that smear life, in the heart like a dubious sad roar. Chororó, guarará, chororó.

But here we are, me and you, Brinks'i, I don't yet know what will become of my *catin* floozy life, here in this beach town of Guaratuba with the oldguy like a castigation. What crap, merdeuse crappy balls. What did I expect? My body in decline, Brinks'mi, the afternoon in decline, Brinks'michĩ, la vie on the wane, Brinks'michĩmi, death, oh, Brinks'michĩmíra'ymi, la mort, that dame of shade and injury, dark and ready, that lady of my pools of existence now that the oldie heads closer to there than here, and above all, with the boy who enflames my core like a rotting rêve of black sin. Quoi to do? Brinks'michĩmíra'ymi.

You, only you, out of the entire universe that begins right here in la sea, michĩeteveva, only you, superior being who dispenses words, grumpy at times, but always Brinks, agate-seahorse, wee bouncing ball, Brinks'michĩmíra'ymi, savageries, delicate steel-chain leash, our promenades along avenues Atlantique and Brazil, our escapes down toward those houses on Prosdócimo Street, your trot in the sand, your panique at unexpected waves, your ordinarily passionate friendship and amitié. Brinks'michĩmi, sudden wish that life keep going, that the morning be one fact among the victories of the day, we have to resist and not give up like the oldguy, and above all that I, dear teeny animal, plush foxarooski, above all that I, your wee tail an agile comma, you child I never had, Brinks, Brinks'i, Brinks'imi, Brinks'michĩ, babytiger, wild, my killer beastie, my diminutive foxy-terrier with pawsies, oh Brinks'michĩmi, your pawsies so teenytiny, michĭeteveva, almost invisible, Brinks'michĭmíra'ymi, so miniscule they seem to belong to a toy of nails and eyeteeth, Brinks'michĭmi, and above all that I, that I, Brinks, Brinks'i, Brinks'michĭ, Brinks'i, that I can't go on any more, Brinks'michĭmíra'ymi.

Where are you? Where was it, if you're no more than a shadow in night's scribble that takes hold of me when I'm utterly alone, Brinks'michĭmíra'ymi, without ever having had you, teenytiniestteeny, you're not nobody, not you, nor the afternoon, and I, I'm so utterly alone: Brinks'michĭmíra'ytotekemi.

This must be the birth of water: drunken, extremely tipsy, a few glasses silvery, others of purest ash. What a farce it is in the beach town if at three in the afternoon everything fries in agony, suffocating sans soleil, the afternoon hot as blazes à Guaratuba, before the Rains let loose. Drunken yes, tipsy yes, but never with the pale hypocrisy of the harpies who shut themselves in mourning and keep their desire to love in the glass cabinets where their ancestors of fog and photo and quicklime move, dance of suspended verre in beveled glass where you can see, even if fleetingly, the suspended drip of the fatal venom, translucent on the goblet lip—like the grizzled old saw that claims living is an astounding thing, and because the heat's crazy and the trees drenched in electricity and the eau d'sea gently ruffles up, this sea, paraná, panamá, the sky leaden and windless, me drunk for the third day, I enter naked into the watery flesh of this sea—wave-lapped as in fairytale islands, sea et sea, drunken I confesse I've lived[10]—je vous avoue que j'ai vécu—these waters, me cursing the bitch putain who gave birth to the mother of that barwoman or ranting at her cuckolded cossack husband in her tawdry wine bar where I almost always inevitably begin my ethylated journeys or, when I least suspect, the terminus nearly irrevocable of these rest stops at cliffs, abymes, jugs of cognac et white vodka meurtrier, one shot après un autre in the town center, me here, null et naked, without punctum or period, avec these tits already sagging to my belly, god suddenly controlling my destiny and the result is I'm as voluminous as a grosse elefant, but never no way did I give up these necessary and irrevocable vices in exchange for the foolishness of aesthetics and whims, like my unhinged drinking of every possible alcoholic breuvage or that other sea—the boy with a Medean and essential fury. And—deplorable j'admets—my meticulous and cultivated irritation at the oldguy as if he'd told me, the wreck, that I'd keep on living, after he'd gone, but with his stubborn vengeance I'd turn, day by day, into the biggest *catin* trollop, the biggest trashy flooze in Guaratuba, and at first I suffered the death of things, the weight, the flaccid tit, but la death of the oldguy, in an irremediable process, tops everything, scandalous

---

10 Refers to Pablo Neruda's memoirs, *Confieso que he vivido*. The English version of Neruda's book is titled simply *Memoirs*.

leader who only through me and with my care could keep on leading and only for as long as I withstood it. With the oldguy gone, I was marafonass over teakettle. The deep truth is that we needed each other and if death for him was pain, for us both it was unbefitting—with him dead our monstrosity'd be alone and dazzled, and if we were to die together before his final full and complete construction, it wouldn't hold up in such swift downfalls, and even the drool would be testament absolu to his regression to l'origine of time. Marafona floozy, yes that's me—I want to yell it at the top of my lungs, but my breath's suffocated by the lapping of this sea, mute and null, but for the weight of my deflagrated corpus, frappé par les waves, and I foresee the lightning and the bestial fury of the thundering thunderstorm, the boiling restlessness of the sea, sky of sinister flashes. It's like orgasme, his body struck and thunderstruck by the sweltering breeze in these waters of auguries and oceans, me drunk and in goosebumps, I wailed for him, for the boy, so as to possess him more than he does me, all waves and pouffiasse désir for sun—semen and water, weddings and dusk, I'd hold him like a giant mothering and immense Macunaimian madonna, Indian, pajé-shaman-prophet, Tupã, me and my tellement crazy glitterings given that, with him, l'ecstase was grabbed emphatically by the orgasm of the sea, rag-doll, *catin*, rising straight to the head, moi the *catin* marafona floozy of this beach town, I vomit it for you, may your seventeen years grab me, you who were born with your face to the sun, mounting mane and bareback, péché et pompe, your thighs and muscles, green glint in your eyes, the serpent, le serpent, the viper. No one to catch sight of us *in flagrante* in this enchantment of sexe on sex, decrepit age versus the jubilant dark blood of those who are, every one, at this very moment, being popped into the earthly profession, moved even if only by the conflagration of their adolescence of deaths and deception. Demain I'll chante a floozy marafona song in arpeggios sad as is the wee glint of eternity; if in the sea all's grieving I am the souveraine madame of the boy—near his skin turned oyster-grey by the sooty smear of time and of the days under the acid bleu of these scalded skies, raining now as if they were bawling all over the beach town and saving us from the tragédie of having no guarantee of surviving when we're wracked by thirst. The water's on fire and I, into the sea, go drunken like those shipwrecked bottles with their messages inside.

All I know is that this living's tiring and I point to the oldguy as the most precise confirmation of this sad fate, achy, this earth burdened by evil and karma, our earth made of disappointments and fright, golden earth calcinated by anguish and the evil hour,[11] this here-and-now that almost makes me die, at each bone of day or at the tail-end of the minute and its embroidered seconds. There's no flourishing in this achy valley achy of achy tears achy.[12] I piss panic into the clock at my life, in all the clocks through which life goes past and walks past and walks and walks and walks et surtout wears out. Achy. L'oldie, even more so than the boy, is guilty. Eighty-five years, on top of all those I never witnessed of his existence sordide et fragile. Now that he won't exist, will no longer ever existe, j'imagine myself in the ache of childbirth and mother, the ache that aches with the sole fact of continuing to live—as if I had no right to such a huge privilege. Our world, I realize, our world is achy and those threads where I pass the needle's meeting extend into hell, aguyje magical aguyje of our new rencontres yet once more. Who knows maybe I'll sleep then mboiraĩhu, mboiraĩhu—silente et unruffled in the throne of the lap of the oldie now but a dove teenytiny and fleeting. No, achy, non, achy. This is what's unbearable at times. From aguyje to aguyje all I'll allow myself is simple contact of the flesh with the sea's water—tupã and not the karai of flamme that tournes us, again et encore, into understandable ashes.

---

11 "La mala hora" refers to a García Márquez story, titled "In Evil Hour" in English.

12 A phrase from the Catholic prayer "Salve Regina": "in this vale of tears."

La fatigue des métals, l'oeuf de l'oegg du scorpion, the lurking, the tacit meat made a yoke, inheritance of our elders, what's spent, les years, moitié ville, moitié vie, the scorched crossing, rivière ébulliante de cinquante winteres, the dark face of exhausted blood, kidneys already failing, la pression artérial, nettle and paprika, the cape or end-point, the sea, le cap, la mer, the facte and the cape of good hope, those lost in the brambles, the fact, the arc du sinistre, les pallid ones, dusk, our chambre, notre maison, ñemomirĩ, the humblest lamp, our bed, the amputated sexe that still itches. And I choke it, the flaccid, le flou, the hollow of the hollowe of the middle, it's all in half-light. And there's worse: demain il faut que je me chante a new zany chanson, and maybe I will feel as complète as all the stations of the Darkest Hour.

Aquidauana, Dorados, Puerto Soledad, cities of rivières and dust, of bones languid at exactly two in the afternoon, sièste et feu, it dumbfounds us febrile in an imponderable viscosité, it all goes sweaty and sucks, it all blanches creamy in a death shudder of innards éclatés plus the gut-ache full of scorn and vomit, the tree does not move tout seul, the taste of sex on the tongue, la langue, le sexe in multiple languages, ayvu, almost like a deflowered rose, death and sex don't talk but how splendide sex feels—the belly that lifts its hackles, resounding tremor of the skin touched par desire and coma, the air, all the air as it was, choked, a thirst that can't be slaked by water and the sudden fear just as, after un peu, le dur soleil could dry out les rues where reign only bordels and bars de port—dead and void from this fatigue de personne et de no-one. Aquidauana. How tristes, how mélancoliques sont les soirs qui s'attardent brûlants et encore mutes, notre maison des femmes, our house of women, on the main drag on the frontière, our bedrooms suffocantes, sheet and sex and cette punishing heat. All of it in ce temps-ci, right now, I can't forget, so it makes up a kind of destiny—a way of suffering less, that God gives us so only today can we recognize cette inclination we have to martyrdom and jubilation. Deux couteaux et two blades. May Thy great hand forever save us so the definitive crystal or its splendid shard doesn't plunge into our souls, in the foam of blood and glass. The sea tinged ruby. Paraîpieté. Pará.

Añaretã.

The inferno of hell's enfer exists and might be the oldguy or might be le boy and mainly it might be this abrupt Sônia Braga of my marafona floozy days and so, staring at the rippling sea of waves and foams in this beach ville in the Paraná, I nearly burst into tears because Brinks can exist in general, precarious negation of hell with which we try to dribble past death, if not its sole affirmation.

The face: non, not le visage of his dead face on the bathroom floor, the suddenly deadguy whom I dragged onto the sofa dans le salon, as mere joke (or yoke?) to get his weight off my conscience, given that the oldie was already no more, the face was that of Sônia Braga so unrelenting in my marafona floozy dream that because of it, yes, because of it I already had abrupt desires for carnage and crime. As far as the oldguy goes, I swear at the foot of the altar of the gods, I'd never do him any harm, no one ever would, given that the oldie was already nearly death just about to happen and thus didn't necessarily need any contribution from our hands.

It was all because of her face, the face of Sônia Braga that I started to weave this étrange slaughter, more perfect than anything is perfect when what's in question is death. I'll weep more than would a mère for the boy as well, now that all turns to grief in this bloodbath, you understand, sir, oh only you understand me, Dr. Paiva. My mer? My mere sea? All sea ici, en soi, c'est moi, merci. It's me. Ĩyá.

*eluci**di**ctionary
of the Guaraní langue

ACHY: nature necessarily mortal, finite and aching world, before getting to the Land of No Evil.

AGUYJE: state of grace that, according to the Guaraní, permits ascension to the Land of No Evil, where the gods live.

AÑARETÃ: hell, enfer.

ANDIRÁIMEVÁ: infernal, something hellish.

ANDIRÁ: bat.

ANDIRÁIMEVÁ: A cloud of bats, a flurry.

ARACATI: day scented by sea air.

ARACUTÍ: flying ant.

ARARIRIĨ: synonym for the previous word, flying ant.

AYVU: the human word, le mot.

MBA: completely; entirely; totality; plenitude; first word of the second letter of the Guaraní alphabet, the consonant *mb*.

MBERÚ: housefly.

MBERUÑARÓ: swarm of flies.

MBOI: cobra.

MBOICHUMBÉ: coral cobra; turn the color of coral.

MBOIHOVĨ: green cobra; to turn green; to turn blue-green.

MBOIRAĨHU: make love.

BRINKS'I: the marafona floozy's expression of affection, which means something like Brinkski. In Portuguese: Brinksinho.

BRINKS'IMI: Brinkski-baby. In Portuguese: Brinksizinho.

BRINKS'MICHĨ: Brinkski-winksy-baby. In Portuguese: Brinksisinhinho.

BRINKS'MICHĨMIRA'YMI: Brinkski-winksky-baby-waby. In Portuguese: Brinksisinhinhozinho.

BRINKS'MICHĨMIRA'ITOTEKEMI:
Brinkskiwinskybabywabyinksybrinksywabyzaby. In Portuguese: Brinksisinhinhozinhozzinozinhozinho.

> NOTE: the endless agglutination of diminutive suffixes coupled to a name, Brinks, creates in Guaraní something so miniscule that it can only be seen through a microscope. It's been turned into something so tiny, almost invisible, that the very text suggests it's something that can't be seen or that, effectively, in this case, *does not exist.*

CATERETÊ: religious dance practiced by early Guaraní peoples.

CHIÃ: noise of boiling water; squeak of a wheel or from the chest, of the respiratory passages; a gasping noise.

CHINÍ: another word that refers to the burbling of water when it boils.

CHORORÓ: murmur; whispering; onomatopoeia for the noise made by placidly running water; equivalent to the popular Brazilian expression *chúa-chúa*. In English: *psst-pssst* (for whispering) or *babbling* (for water).

CUÑÁ: woman.

CUÑAMBATARÁ: prostitute, fallen woman, marafona floozy, catin, trollop, pouffiasse.

CURURU: spiritual or religious dance of the early Guaraní, also known as a *cateretê*.

GUARARÁ: noise like rain or water; sound of a swarm of insects; noise of what suddenly falls.

HETAICOÉ: very many of them; many exist; there are very many.

HOVĨ: green; really a bluish green or greenish blue, in European culture.

HOVĨ-HOVĨ: to turn green; to turn blue greenly and greenly blue.

ĨGUASU: sea, mer, mar.

ĨPAGUASÚ: synonym for the previous word: sea.

ITACUPUPÚ: boiling or burbling water.

ĨYÁ: aquatic god of the Guaraní; the *duende* or spirit of water.

JAGUARA: Jaguar, puppy (affectionately speaking).

JAGUARÁ: Third person singular of "jaguar," to wander or gad about, hang around.

JAGUAPITÃ: vermillion, reddish or purplish puppy; city in the north of Parana, near Londrina.

JAGUARAÍVA: name given to a puppy that is useless for hunting; mongrel: city in the north of Paraná, its name is slightly altered—*Jaguariaíva.*

KARAI: prophets who announced to the Guaraní the need to seek the Land of No Evil; flame; solar flare; heat; rebirth; is opposed to (and completes) Tupã.

MICHĨ: small; miniscule; minor; suffix that indicates a diminutive.

MICHĨETEVEVÁ: infinitely small; super-infinitely small; (almost) invisible thing.

MONGETÁ: love, to make love.

MORANGU: legend; fable; tale.

ÑANDU: spider; also, the verb "to feel" and the noun "feeling."

ÑANDUCAVAYÚ: spider of the tarantula family.

ÑANDUGUASÚ: ostrich.

ÑANDUTÍ: fine weaving or brocade, a traditional Paraguayan lace; from a word for web of a small spider.

ÑANDURENIMBÓ: spider web.

ÑANDUTIMICHĨ: spider webbing; tiny web of a tiny spider.

ÑE'Ẽ: word; vocable; language; idiom; voice; communication; to communicate; to speak; to converse.

ÑEMOMIRĨHÁ: humility.

ÑEMOMIRĨ: humiliation; to be humiliated.

ÑEMONGUETA: conversation, interview, discussion.

OGUERA-JERA: that which unfolds itself in its own unfolding; something that manifests itself in its own manifestation; the fold of the fold of the fold.

PANAMÁ: place of many fish.

PARÁ: sea (in old Guaraní); hue of several colors; polychromatic spaces.

PARANÁ: river that runs to the sea; river the size of a sea, river that is reminiscent of the sea, river that crosses to the sea.

PARAGUAY: precolonial name of Asunción, capital of Paraguay.

PARAÎPÎETÉ: the abyss of the sea.

PI'Á: heart.

PI'AMBERETÉ: strong heart.

PORÃ: pretty; beautiful; handsome; pleasant; the word is both adjective and adverb.

PORÃITÉ: very pretty; beautiful.

PORÃITEREÍ: exceptionally pretty or beautiful.

PORENÓ: copulate; ejaculate; make love.

PUCÚ: broad; tall and slim.

SURUVU: Guaraní myth in which the word becomes a bird.

TAHIĨ: ant.

TAHIĨGUAICURÚ: ant, one of the Ecitonini, an Eciton crassicorn ant.

TAĨHU: love.

TAPIÁ: forever.

TASĨ: ache; be in pain; suffer pain; sickly; ill; illness; pain; sickness.

TAVA: village.

TAVAIGUÁ: native village.

TIEGUI: lower abdomen.

TINĨ: noise of water boiling.

TECOVÉ: life, vie, person, persona, personne.

TECOVEMBIKI: short life.

TECOVEPÁ: cease living; give up life.

TECOVEPAVAERÃ: mortal.

TUCÚ: grasshopper.

TUGUĨVAÍ: bad blood; downtrodden blood; sick blood.

TUPÃ: Supreme Being; opposed to *Karai;* absolute god of the world's waters, and of the world itself.

TUPAITÁ: rock of God.

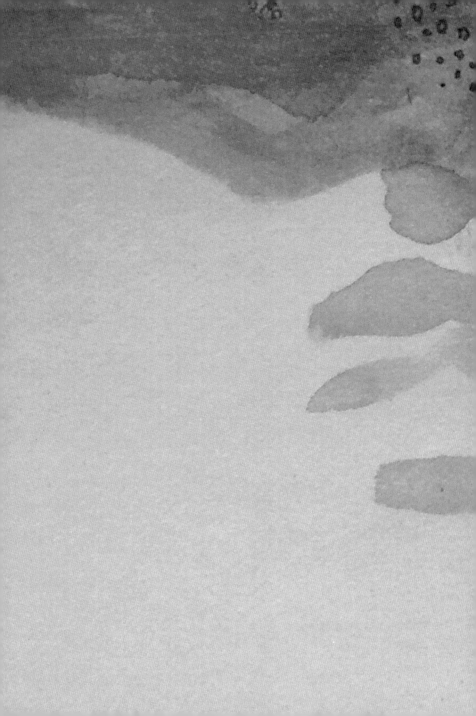

Paranalumen,
a mixelated Portunholçaisupí postface

Andrés Sjens (Chile)
glabberfasted into *mourE(orless)nglish*

> —Uma vez puso dos ingleses nocaute en la calhe!
> Pasavam e mi daban encontrones todavia! Yo me fui
> arrabiando e exclame: —Animales! Hijos de puêta! Se
> volvieron luego diez ou doce! Mas antes de fechar el
> tiempo, dê al primeiro uno swing en la nariz, al segundo
> un chochet em la padaria. Fuemos todos parar en el
> pau. Se reía de mi muque el jefe de Polizia! E me invito
> para instrutor de Box de sua famijia!
>
> (An Argentinian secretary speaking portunhol in
> Oswald de Andrade's *Serafim Ponte Grande,* 1933)

Paraná's not for nada. It's Argentinian city, of
course, and Brazilian state, but long before that, at its
tangled Tupi-Guaraní roots, it's river: a *río* that springs
northwest of Río and twice becomes a fluid border
(Paraguayan-Brazilian, Paraguayan-Argentinian) before
flinging itself, southern, into the mouth of the Plata.
And it is the river that flows in "the poetry of the prose-
ator" Wilson Bueno (to echo Bonvicino). Not for nada:
something truly flowing conjures and/or conjugates in
the liquid coming and going through that meridianal co-
marquing. Something, yes, lets itself be seen—sniffed?—

from the start, not entirely absurd and, all in all, almost, insignificant.

A time ago, compelled by a pair of fluvial editors of cutting-edge philosophy, I fell into a trance translating a "French" text by an (un)known co-markable writer who, in one consummate passage, dated precisely in February 1986, has us read of a singular "experience on the banks of the Paraná." Upstream from Rosario, the Paraná River's south bank makes itself out to be a sort of Latin-American *rive gauche*, as Raul Bopp mentioned in *Cobra Norato* (1931), a *Nheengatu* (legend, tale) *of the southern reaches of Amazonia*. Experience of the *before* of written (European) History: a *before* the before of the "after" (the Spanish Conquest), a before without Western future, without Greek "gift" horse and, to be more precise, we'll spell out its name: *The Heights of Macchu-Picchu* (Felstiner, William Little, etc.).

On the other bank, just as *bueno*, on the other and northern side of the Paraná, do I need to list? we can find the less huge *Macunaíma* (1928), by the Brazilian Mario de Andrade, an oldnew story written earthily by a shapeshifting parrot, and Bopp's *Cobra Norato*, hot flowing current already mentioned, tidal bore and tail of prior springwaters.

Paraguayan Sea, in any case, from its first appearance in 1992, is not (just take a look-see) of either side of the river: it is a motley mixture, as Néstor Perlongher puts it in his tasty "Paraguayan Soup," or "paraîpieté" as Wilson Bueno writes in the *Sea* itself. In this poematical story, what it is that the river "is," river that rides along on itself, great Tupi-Guaraní sea-river (*paraná*, in the Guaraní eluci*dict*ionary), is the profusion of waters, sea of river, river com-penetrating sea, riversea; as such, in the northeast, in Pernambuco and Paraíba— oh liana of my Liliana, ayahuasca. *Paraguayan Sea*, as I was saying, is an anticipatory ride of the kind that, with others, persistently dots the marafonic warp and weave of the oeuvre of Wilson Bueno. His *Meu Tio Roseno, a Cavalo* (2000) fine-tunes the name and, unusually, the digestion of what is perhaps the summit work dividing the waters from the far side of northern desert: Guimarães Rosa, *Grande Sertão: Veredas* (1956). *Meu Tio* takes up the familial saga at the exact point where *Paraguayan Sea* leaves off, which is to say: at the point at which one and the other bank of the river can no longer be distinguished, hung up in the web of three (un)borders. Moreso than in the Rosa-Nerudian *margins of happiness*, then, and even before *A terceira margem do rio* ("The Third Bank of the River," in Guimarães Rosa's *Primeiras Estórias*, 1962) that, at every point unreservedly wanders everywhere and does not Rosa (or rise) anywhere—it's lively, this river.

From his south bank, Neruda becomes adjective in *Paraguayan Sea*—an adjective that, all considered, and alongside Tupi-Guaraní, is *essential*. Neruda, a certain Neruda: he of the defeats of *Veinte poemas de amor* (1924) and memoirist of *Confieso que he vivido* (1974), expressly convoked by the marafonic hubris of Guaratuba in Bueno's story, the narrating "I" with its singular letter. Neruda's own story is that of the "inflation of the I," according to Enrique Lihn, of the romantic and "neo-romantic Latin-American" and macho (old or not): his suicidal carnage, apparent bit by bit, is also essential, as is all romanticism, Latin-American or not, and interminably. "Guaraní is as essential to this story as the flight of the birrd, the speck on the window, the cooing of French or the cascade of Nerudaesque outpourings in a single seule suicide of capacious English words." And if there is more than one Neruda, if "Neruda"—his cadaver or remains, his textual body—is not totalizable, and if there is more than one Neruda on the southern bank of the Paraná, that of the "before" of the "after" of History, *Paraguayan Sea* is the other, then, or the least other among others, for Bueno's northern echo is enamored and infinitisimally oedipal. (Neruda and Mallarmé, Eliot, Rilke, García Márquez and, among others, Lorca singing marafonically at exactly five in the afternoon, all put in literary appearances in Bueno's story, which is in some

ways a homage to reading itself.) In the doggyish Brinks':
and even sans Brinks': Wilson Bueno, between one brink
and another, is seafully desirous between the before of
the "before" and the after of the "after." Between one
time and another, one time and every other: Paraná is the
pit-stop of shipwrecked desire without limits or borders
— a *poemarafo*.

In Bueno's *Pequeño Tratado de Brinquedos* (1996)
there's a poem which he often liked to quote:

> me and my mistress
> go out to hunt brushes
> and only catch crickets
>
> come back late and famished
> and dine on our names (*anonymous*)

Which is to say: in mid-water, in the river navigat-
ed to the extreme and steaming—not the pale hypocrisy
of grandes dames ostentatiously mourning with their de-
sires for love shut in glass cabinets—lies a Paraguayan sea
in its mar/sea/mer/phonic drink, as might be found in
shipwrecked bottles holding messages: monstroous, the
double "o" of that marine tooth and/or morose remains,
a monstrosity that needs not ostentate but, not for nada,
ostentates itself ostentating monstrously, oyster ostra
*h*ostage onstage.

The anonymous name of the monstroous marafona in *Paraguayan Sea* is, I'll hazard a guess, an *Agôalumem*, Agualumen, "that marine aerial monster capable of flying high and splashing intact into the watery drink, just as night falls into the high sea" that appears, in frankly portuguese-resplendence, in Bueno's *Jardim Zoológico* (1999): the agualumbre, vagalumen and aqualux, who intervenes to translate one zoo of signs into another:

> "And there are tales *[this translated for you from the French! of Ajens who translates from the Brazilian of the zooish Bueno]* of nightmarish nights, nights now five centuries old, when the mariners, dreaming aloud, call out, incessant, from their bunks, for l'ôlumen, that marvel... "oh marvel," "oh-seas unceasing", "oh sea see-n," "oh marvelous"

Santiago de Chile, February–March 2001, etc.

Paraguayan Sea and the *Marafona* Floozy of Guaratuba

Christian Kent
Paraguayan poet born Asunción, 1983
Translated from Spanish by Erín Moure

When I started reading *Paraguayan Sea,* I imagined that the word "marafona" ("marafona floozy" in English, "trollop" at times, and "catin" and "pouffiasse" in French) came from the cascade of Bueno's own unhindered "ayvu" (words, human language). To me, it meant mar-(a)fona, literally an a-phonic sea, silent sea, sea (without) noise. Not content with this, I sought *marafona* in the Portuguese Wikipedia, and after discarding the names of famed soccer players, I found: *"The marafona is a rag doll, without eyes, nose or ears, dressed in a colorful local costume. Its skeleton is a cross of wood, wrapped in cloth."*

It continued: *"During the celebration, brides-to-be dance with the marafonas. After the party, the dolls are left on top of the bed where they have the power to rid the house of storms and lightning, and of the evil eye. On the wedding day, they're put under the bed (since they have no eyes or ears or mouth, they see nothing, hear nothing, and can't tell the tale) to bring fertility to the marriage. The marafonas are associated with the cult of fertility."*

Etymologically, the word "marafona" comes from the Arabic "mara haina," "trickster woman." Given this, a marafona can also be a prostitute, a "cuñambatará" in Guaraní, or a "loose, disheveled, kelembú woman." [Note from EM: thus "trollop" in English with its echo of "dollop" and "gallop," and "catin" in French, a Quebec word meaning prostitute, doll, country bumpkin girl and bandaid.] Essentially, though, it is a woman who deceives or who has tricks up her sleeve ("to those of you who read me as if you were discreetly pressed to the crack of a shut door") or turns tricks. [13]

This marafona floozy-*catin* is the narrator of *Paraguayan Sea*, and her multifaceted meanings might be missed without my clarification. This marafona of Guaratuba, a "cuñambatará," a rag doll without a face, an erotic symbol, a turner of tricks irremediably tied to a decrepit old man and linked to the mysterious fog surrounding his death, tells a confessional tale, deployed in circles like a kind of ritual dance, turning on one repeated fact in a macaber game that is also comical and, at times, metaphysical. Bueno's diminutive, agglutinative, excessive and microscopic linguistic tide of Guaraní keeps construct-ing a symbolic universe teeming with debates on death, sickness ("tasy"), life's transience ("tecovembiki"), the divine ("tupã"),

---

13 EM note: Marafonas or matrafonas exist as dolls in Portugal, too, and at Carnaval time they can be men who dress up as women. There, the word is seen to come from vocables meaning "mother earth." Curiously there is an assonance as well with *marihuan*a.

the infernal ("añaretãmeguá"), the sexual ("porenó"), imagination ("morangú"), love ("mboiraĩhu") and literature ("ñandurenimbó"—spider web).

The limits of the world itself are truly the limits of this strange, mythical "yopará" or Paraguayan mixelation, this epistemological "Paraguayan soup" as the late Néstor Perlongher had it, and these limits are delineated by the poetic consciousness of the floozy of Guaratuba, the poet-transvestite turned into a funny *catin* without a face who, in pursuing the hypotheses for her crime, pursues her very identity.

> I'm my own construction et ainsi je me considère the first to blame for all the fallen scaffolding of my attempted projet. Will I find myself? Je ne sais pas et I persevere, as best I can: writing my story down even if it gives me shooting douleurs in my ovaries et un saut in the pulse of a vein near my heart.

Paraguayan Sea is a confession. The marafona floozy of Guaratuba wants above all to claim her innocence regarding the death of the oldguy; "No, believeyoume, I speak truly: I didn't kill the oldie." But the trap set by the spidery tarantula of a tale ("ñandu, ñanducavayú, ñandutí") keeps growing and extends outward until everything falls into it. The confession here is not just a proclamation of innocence but the emergence, from its tale, of all the possible becoming of language and words; this language that creates itself for and by itself as the tale evolves, keeps inventing ("oguera-jera" like the tutelary father of the cosmogenic Mbyá) and can only refer to the mysteries that it in itself contains. *Paraguayan Sea* is a "marafona language," a *catin* trickster floozy without a face, "cuñambatará," oceanic and millimetric all at once, with the mission, it seems, of holding tight to ordinary life.

A Guaraní agglutination combining everything into a single kilometric word, *Paraguayan Sea* acts as a life-saving spell: "I write so that my heartstrings don't snap dedans."

Ñemongueta:

An interview with Wilson Bueno by Claudio Daniel
Translated from Portuguese by Erín Moure

Fables written in the shadowy border between lived experienced and dream, the work of Wilson Bueno is a vast mythology that seduces us with its playfulness. At once allegory and a tropical stew that mixes languages and cultures both high and low, the fiction of this unusual author configures a mixelated and mixblooded baroque. Like all great literature, it transcends mere verbal architecture and seeks to comprehend the human adventure. Its author, Wilson Bueno, born in 1949 in the city of Jaguapitã, in the interior of the Paraná region of Brazil, has published many other novels, including: *Bolero's Bar* (1986), *Manual de Zoofilia* [*Bestiality Manual*] (1991), *Mar Paraguayo* [*Paraguayan Sea*] (1992), *Cristal* [*Crystal*] (1995), *Jardim Zoológico* [*Zoo*] (1999), *Meu Tio Roseno, a Cavalo* [*My Uncle Roseno on Horseback*] (2000), *Amar-te a ti nem sei se com carícias* [*Love Yourself With or Without Caresses*] (2004), *Cachorros do céu* [*Sky Dogs*] (2005) and *A copista de Kafka* [*The Kafka Copyist*] (2007), as well as two books of poetry, *Pequeno Tratado de Brinquedos* [*Brief Treatise on Toys*] (1996) and *Pincel de Kyoto* [*Kyoto Paintbrush*] (2008). For eight years, Bueno also edited the legendary literary magazine *Nicolau*, a landmark in the history of Brazilian cultural journalism.

Claudio Daniel:
You were born in Jaguapitã, a small city 50 km from Londrina, in the Paraná province of Brazil. Are memories of your birthplace, of tales heard in childhood, present in your books? In what way?

Wilson Bueno:

Most certainly. Tales invented (or reinvented) by aunts, grandparents, and above all by my mother, an excellent storyteller, are present in my writing and, by extension, in all my books, even those with a radical aesthetics, if I can put it that way. For me, the imagination is always the happy condensation of this mix of experience and personal mythology. We are forever telling stories about others, even though these stories are actually profoundly ours and don't really come from others because we discover them first...

Your prose fiction employs the resources of poetic text, such as sound games, startling images, and linguistic inventions, and the results are like living emeralds. Where does prose end and poetry begin?

It's all the art of poetry. That's how I write, and always have. I don't know how to write without being intimate. Prose retains and is generated by poetry, in a process that aspires firstly to be free. Literature, to me, is the maximum liberty that we enjoy on Earth—and I want to flourish in the love of writing, the epiphanic pleasure of its glow. I can't write if I'm divided and held back by the canon and by norms. It's in the exasperating space of freedom where I must situate myself in order to be effective. And it's all poetry. Living in itself is a poetic act, as Hölderlin wrote. And everyone agrees that, of all the poetic acts, the one which demands the most courage, bravery, heroism, is what might be called fearlessness. It's indispensable if we are to survive the perplexity in which we are caught alive.

In some of your novels, there are quotes from Guaraní, from the lexicon and the imaginary of Guaraní, often mixed with or transfigured by your own linguistic confabulations. When did you begin to be interested in Indigenous culture? Did you study Indigenous folklore?

No, I don't have Indigenous expertise, shall we say. My curiosity regarding this theme, paradoxically, precedes my own appearance as a self. I was born in the backwoods, at a time—it wasn't long ago that the Paraná had backwoods—when virgin forest and almost untouched native fauna existed. My great-grandfather was part Guaraní; he married a German. Imagine that mixture. My great-grandmother (my maternal grandmother's mother) was courted in rural Saõ Paulo state by another German with glittery blue eyes. I paid homage to this great-grandfather in *Tio Roseno* and, clearly, obviously, to my Guaraní great-grandmother. To me, indigeneity and indigenous space are almost a second skin; I am anxious and perplexed in the midst of boulevard trees, automobiles, traffic.

How would you describe your creative process? Do you write daily? Do you hatch the plot first, or does the narrative evolve in the act of writing? How do characters emerge? Does language itself drive the growth of the tale, or do words emerge from the rhythm of the narrative?

Strangely, I don't even think of myself as writing. The whole time I'm just haranguing myself and taxing myself, yet there I am, indeed, writing, writing, writing... in notepads, notebooks, agendas, on scraps of paper, napkins. And when I am not writing, I am thinking about what to write, how to write it, in which way I might write. And at the same time, I constantly hang out with my pals, forgetting that Literature exists, and criticizing myself for not writing. I am an Olympian of laziness, one that toils night and day. But maybe I've found a gentler way of engaging in the profession—I keep writing without great pretensions apart from creating things that give me the huge satisfaction of feeling that I've, oh I don't know, captured the improbable...

Jorge Luis Borges once said literature comes from literature, from the infinite ocean of language. Do you agree with that old wizard? Are there books and authors who have marked your growth as a writer?

I completely agree with Borges, for whom literature only made sense if it was enrapt. It was he who advised us to abandon, right off the bat, and definitively, books that don't give us pleasure, which is to say, those that don't enrapt us. There've been many overwhelming influences in my life, up to now, because I keep falling hopelessly in love with new old writers (Ovid, recently). And among writers, I'll name, randomly and in no particular order, Clarice Lispector, Guimarães Rosa, Franz Kafka, Machado de Assis, Borges, Joyce, Cortázar, Cortázar and Cortázar, as well as Hemingway, Gide, Shakespeare, and Calvino and Calvino and Calvino, our master. Then there's all that rotten, perfidious, and amazing Argentinian literature— from Madariaga to Lamborghini, from César Aira to Néstor Perlongher. And my Brazilian contemporaries— Noll, Bernardo Carvalho, Nassar, Hatoum—princes of Brazilian prose...

Meu Tio Roseno a Cavalo, just published, is a novel set in the borderlands of Paraná, Mato Grosso do Sul and Paraguay, amidst battles between armed gangs which you call the Paranavaí War. Please tell us a bit more about this work.

I always find it constricting to talk about a book that's already written and published. All I can say is *there it is; the tale is told*. Anything I can add is redundant, variations on a theme. Or maybe I should just repeat what I wanted to say, as if I didn't manage to say it in the book, as it was too hard to convey. What I can say about *Meu Tio Roseno*, is that of all my books, it was the most thought out, the most planned. I even drew maps to demarcate the humble uncle's route from the foothills of the Amabaí to the gullies of the Paranapanema. And maybe I can add, too, that the book is an expression of my desire to touch the molecular root of narrative, which is the fable. It's a clear, simple, limpid book. Any high-school student can decipher its weft, even if it holds keys, "traps," and "citations" that only obsessive readers manage to grasp. It's all in there—from Greek mythology to Yoruban Candomblé animism, from hillbilly dress-up to soap-operatic guesses, from Verlaine to Baudelaire, with the Brazilian Parnassian poets and "pulp literature" thrown in, like that which the Argentinians, our neighbors, produce so prodigiously...

In *Paraguayan Sea*, you mix Portuguese, Spanish, and Guaraní in a parodic and polyphonic writing, in a mixelated baroque. Is the confluence of linguistic universes symbolic of the "Heinz 57" of Brazilian culture, that has assimilated so many different seasonings? Is it a sign of proximity to the Spanish-American world?

It's all that. You might say that *Paraguayan Sea* holds a mirror to the democracy and proliferation of languages. It is a response to classical rigor, to the straightjackets of literary creation imposed on us before we ever start. With *Sea*, I wanted to break free of all that, anxiety of influence included, by mixing everything into one literary soup, Joyce and Puig, José de Alencar and Machado, Neruda and Octávio Paz. The book is, to me, a declaration of love for literature, of the pleasure in making literature. In any case, I think, and it's true we're the worst judges of our own work, my books express or try to express the joy (which does not dispense with anxiety) of making literature, of digging the most precious jewels out of rough stone.

The text is a monologue that mixes erudite and pop, cabaret and melodrama, and Joycean stream of consciousness. Is this fusion an attempt to break down, within the limitations of textual discourse, the borders between cultural repertoires?

I think that's true. My answer to your last question tried to elaborate on this. The multiplicity of discourses and repertoires in *Paraguayan Sea* is, to me, a full exercise of the "democracy" I mentioned earlier, but it's worth repeating. It's the experience of the diverse at the heart of diversity; it's migrancy (broadly speaking and metaphorically), geographical indetermination (expressed even in the title, for Paraguay, as we know, has no sea—the Paraguayan "sea" where the story takes place is the beach town of Guaratuba, in Paraná, Brazil—um... story?), ambiguity, the contaminating and contaminated mix of languages and it's also a prose-en-abyme. All this has made *Paraguayan Sea* the most loved and studied of all my books. It did shatter the molds, yes, if you'll excuse me the vanity of talking about myself...

What about *Cristal*? What role does it play in your oeuvre?

Curiously, *Cristal* didn't attract much critical attention. As far as reviews go, if I remember right, there was a laudatory and very lucid one by Jairo Arco e Flecha, and another, brilliant, by Jamil Snege, and that was it. Even so, it's a book that circulates, for example, in the Hispanic community in New York, and in blurry xerox copies. Its readers are all trying to tame the tangle of our language to grasp the story of the Oldwoman and her "angel" Ananias, who was dressed as a girl for six christly years because of a religious promise. It's a sad book, if you ask me, profoundly sad, almost desperate. Not even pathos saves it, as it's missing the irrepressible humor that melodrama brings, for example, to *Paraguayan Sea*. In this sense, it clashes with *Sea*. It has no melodrama, only "drama," and by limiting itself to "drama," it has more "class," we might say, but is a dead loss in terms of humor. I love *Cristal*; it's a book for which I have great affection, and I'll never write anything like it again, though I do really like the Faulknerian aura that I think I evoked in the story. Or tried to evoke.

Manual de Zoofilia is a collection of short stories, or prose poems, characterized by metaphorical density, melodic constructions and syntactical ruptures. In it, you've created a teratology with animais as the figures in a discourse on sexual passion. How did this book emerge?

I always wanted to fuse, in a single imagined space, the grapheme "animal" with human sexual passion. *Manual de Zoofilia* points out how much irrationality exists in our discourse of love. To give voice to this irrationality, I sought out examples in animals of charm and sordidity, greatness and knavery, so as to transubstantiate them, if I can use that pedantic word, out of hornyness, copulation, and the vicious and vice-ridden passion through which we humans love each other, at times out of darkest hatred.

In *Jardim Zoológico*, you created another bestiary of fables about imaginary creatures. Incidentally, in the epigraph, Augusto Monterroso states that writers must "take up again, each in accordance with their talent, the task of invention that started with Aesop." Why write fables, today?

To confabulate is to go beyond history, history with an H, demarcated and demarcating, that hoards dates and spacings, both factual and militant. In fable, literary epiphany is consummated and fulfilled. Fabulous and confabulating—from Shakespeare (*A Midsummer Night's Dream*) to Italo Calvino (*The Baron in the Trees*), to name two of my favorites, fable gives a magical quality to literature. There is a primeval innocence in fable and in it is the original magic of the venerable literary art.

Your narrative poem *Os Chuvosos* [*The Rainy Ones*, 1999] was published as a children's book. Will you write more for children?

I've not really thought about it. But I can say that I intended *Os Chuvosos* for readers from 0-100 years old. That's how the book was received, too, even though there were barely 50 copies, handmade singly, as if engravings. People of all ages loved it. But the book also had the magical touch of Jussara Salazar, whose design literally reinvented my text and made it glow on paper.

To change the subject somewhat, you founded and edited the literary magazine *Nicolau*, benchmark of an era, which won prizes in Brazil and abroad. Could you talk a bit about that experience?

Nicolau is a very long story. I like to claim that our small team (Fernando Karl, Joba Tridente, Angelo Zorek) was the last bastion of romantic Brazilian journalism. We made the magazine by hand and succeeded in gathering work from the last of a generation of Brazilian intellectuals, from Millôr to Haroldo de Campos, from Adélia Prado to Hilda Hilst. *Nicolau* was a great moment in Brazilian intellectual life. As the *Jornal do Brasil* classified it, in a memorable full-page article, it was the most authentic "carnival of ideas" in the country at the time. We won every prize, we dared, quarreled, polemicized, sputtered, and from one battle to the next we managed to hang on for eight uninterrupted years of national circulation. One story, just to demonstrate that the battle was worth it: I was visited the other day by a guy around 20 years old from Rio Grande do Sul, a journalism student who was writing a paper on *Nicolau* to present in class. I was very happy when he told me, in short, that his was the second generation to read *Nicolau*. They only knew of the publication via archives, yet their love of the magazine matched that of the first generation of readers. I have heard that all 56 issues of *Nicolau* would be made available online, but I don't know if it's been done. [NOTE: See bibdig.biblioteca.unesp.br/handle/10/25118]

What's exciting in Brazilian literature now? Any new authors of interest?

Brazilian literature has always been exciting. A country that's produced, just to mention two names, Machado de Assis and Guimarães Rosa, is a country with a great literature. There are many people writing seriously in this country, thinking big, despite the ratatouille of literary politics that niggles and fritters away, without ethics or aesthetics. The ratatouille has no time to make literature and only makes ratogens, like pathogens...

Your *Pequeno Tratado de Brinquedos* holds poems that dialogue with the tanka, a Japanese poetic form of 5 lines, related to haiku. Will you publish more books of poetry?

No. I have no intention of putting out a new book of poetry, strictly speaking. I consider *Pequeno Tratado* to be the sum and summary of my poetic output. I wanted to pay homage to one of the founts of poetry—the Orient. It was the book on which I worked the longest: a year and a half to write 58 tankas, barely, each one with but five lines. Only God knows how hard it was. I still have about 25 tankas that did not appear in the book, and one day I'll perhaps publish them as a chapbook called *Pincel de Kyoto*. But, to return to your question, I'm not thinking about writing another book of poetry any time soon.

Cuban poet José Kozer, together with Roberto Echavarren and Jacobo Sefamí, edited the Latin-American anthology *Medusário* [*Medusary*], which included Brazilian writers such as yourself and Haroldo de Campos. Do you think it's time we had more interactions between Brazilian and Latin-American literatures?

The inclusion of 18 pages of *Paraguayan Sea* in *Medusário*, published in Mexico City by the Fondo de Cultura Económica and distributed in all Spanish-speaking countries, was a great honor for me, and still is. It's a rigorous anthology. The other Brazilians in it are Paulo Leminski and Haroldo de Campos. Of course there should be more exchanges between our literatures. The separation of Brazil and Spanish-speaking Latin America has been huge, but recently I've felt that the situation is improving, especially with the internet and with laudable initiatives to bring writers together, such as that of Luis Bravo in Uruguay, and, more recently, of Jorge Montesinos and Douglas Diegués in Asunción, Paraguay. And I have to mention Reynaldo Jiménez as well, the brilliant and generous Argentinian poet and guiding light of Tsé-Tsé, which has published 30 Brazilian poets to date.

Translated and published with the permission of Claudio Daniel. Originally published in 2000 in the *Suplemento Literário de Minas Gerais*, Brazil; republished in June 2010 in Portuguese at: paraguaytamaguxi.blogspot.ca/2010/06/um-nemongueta-com-wilson-bueno.html

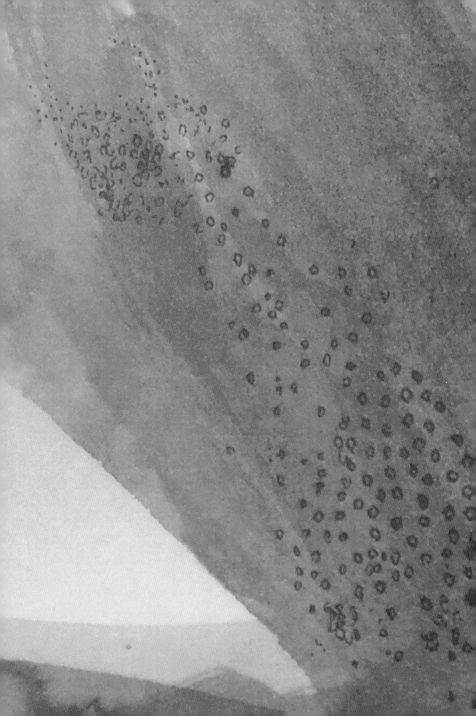

River to the Sea
A commentary by Erín Moure

Mar Paraguayo by the late Brazilian writer Wilson Bueno is a book whose original irrepressibly, irrigorously and irreverently does not comply with immigration regulations. It is in Portunhol or Portuñol, a border mixture of Spanish and Portuguese from a place where Brazil and Argentina touch Paraguay, mixed with Guaraní, a language that long precedes colonial borders and that keeps erupting in the text, an irrepressible vehicle of thought about ontology and sex and the divine. Key to the book is the relation of these three languages and their malleabilities, tensions and temptations, their *tensilities*, and the rhythms that bind them. A translation must not only attend to semantic values, but to this rhythmic binding, through which the "meaning" or meaning effects of Bueno's text are conducted.

The book is a sublime love story, a story that moves in gender traversals, *travestias*. It is a homage to life, a story *of the fact of being embodied*. Who is this narrating woman from Paraguay in a beach town in Brazil, a woman who has loved two men, old and young? Is the narrator really a woman, or of fluctuating gender, or simply a gay man calling himself a woman in that old-fashioned way of gay men? The whole book is a *mar paraguayo*, not a still body of endless horizon, but a moving Paraguayan river-to-the-sea of identities and shifts of phonic sea-mphonics on a hot day in December (Brazilian summer) or cold day in June (winter) on the Brazilian-Atlantic shore, in the beach town of Guaratuba, a place where the beach is often called the Paraguayan Sea as Paraguayans flock there for summer vacations. Paraguay, with its Guaraní and Spanish, its riverations and reverberations, crosses all borders. We readers don't know if the marafona, the faceless speaking doll, the loose woman or floozy of the book, speaks Guaraní because she, too, once migrated from Paraguay to the beach, then stayed, or if she is a native of Guaratuba and has absorbed the Guaraní words from tourists in her own surroundings. The book is a displacement of a displacement and a homage to displacements. It is a story worth reading in English purely for this, but also for its rhythms and undulations, its vascularity and mimesis and shiftings, its impossibility of being pinned down, its celebration of the miniscule Brinks, our animality, our ability to emerge in playful leaping (Brinks could come from "brincar") and disappear just as quickly in a quirky excess of syllables that marks both invisibility and infinity. Oh, no, *Paraguayan Sea* can't be pinned down, except to say, and this, surely: we only thrive through the tiniest of gestures, the most miniscule; these sustain us— and we only thrive through the grandest gesture and loss of borders of all, which is to say: through love.

In 2003, I translated two small excerpts for the *Oxford Book of Latin American Poetry* (2009), turning Bueno's Portunhol infused with Guaraní into "Franglawk," combining English, French and Kanien'kehá (Mohawk), the main languages in the place where I did the translation (Montreal). Though Bueno and others urged me to continue, I was able to sustain the cadence only for a few pages. I did not have the resources then to help with Kanien'kehá, and online dictionaries were minimal at the time; I did not want to the Kanien'kehá language foolishly, from outside, to "stand in" for the Guaraní.

In attending to the tensilities and rhythms between the trio of Bueno's languages, I wanted a northern version of his *Paraguayan Sea* that would be trilingual/admixtured but still readable in English. My invented *Frenglish*, an English containing French, is inspired by Quebec English, but intensified. It's not really readable in French, just in English, whereas Bueno's Portunhol is quite readable in Spanish and fairly readable in Portuguese. The indigenous language proved more difficult. Guaraní is co-official in Paraguay, very much alive in the area where Portunhol is spoken, primarily where Paraguay, Argentina, and Brazil meet. The language has a closer relationship or cohabitation to Portuguese and Spanish speakers there than do any of the indigenous languages of Canada with French and English speakers in our day. In the past, such relationships did exist, and English and French—until the early 20th century—absorbed words of Cree and Anishinaabe, Nsilxcín and Dane-zaa, Siksika and other languages, as people dealt, separately and together, with the specificities of the lands of Turtle Island, what we know as North America. But the forced removal, throughout much of the Canadian twentieth century, of First Nations children to residential schools, where they were starved and beaten into "assimilation," acted to break generational transmission of language. A minor effect of this great and genocidal loss to indigenous peoples was that the direct and equal contacts between indigenous languages and English/French were also severed.

Now, post-residential-school and post-official-apology-for-residential-schools, there is a lot of catching up to do just so that people can rebuild the generational transmission of their languages. Because of this, use of an indigenous language from the North in a literary project from the South that in fact belongs to the European/

colonial tradition is a fraught issue, and cannot simply and blindly be assumed. Languages are not there for us to simply *use*, at times. Why should a threatened language of Canadian spaces want to be in an unusual melee of a confessional novel by a Brazilian from Paraná, translated by a Canadian poet from Quebec? What is serving whom and how here? Whose identity is here spaced, spaced out, interspaced?

I decided to trust Bueno's own admonition that Guaraní is essential to the text, for Guaraní bursts out of his text at every seam, even the most infinitesimal, and its epistemologies and relations are crucial. With his Guaraní and my invented Frenglish, I worked to respect the eerie and gorgeous undulations of Bueno's poetic prose, and create a text that allows an English speaker, I hope, to read the beauty and radicality of what Wilson Bueno did. It may be easier to read for a Canadian speaker, exposed to French. As for other North American and cross-Atlantic English speakers, they'll find it a bit more mysterious, but will fall into its rhythm, I think.

Unavoidably, then, my translation does oblige English-speaking readers of *Paraguayan Sea* to confront unreadability in a way that the *Portunharaní* original does not. Spanish and Portuguese, in their close linguistic proximity, work synchronically in Bueno's text, alongside each other, keeping time moving in the same direction, while Guaraní interrupts rhythmically, and also sends readers to the dictionary at the back (making the book a real "page turner," a kinetic sculpture that includes our hands) to grasp meanings. The book has to be held in the hands, moved: the body interrupts the unfolding of the narrative by leaping pages to reach the dictionary, over and over again. In *Paraguayan Sea*, however, because English and French are less close, they don't always operate synchronically but diachronically, breaking up the movement of time, and the rhythm as well.

Paraguayan Sea, I hope, provides one answer to the question of how to create in the "no traducir," in the "ne pas traduire," which is to create in synchronicity with translation's *mise en abyme* or *entre-lugar,* its open spacings which are one with its possibility. And no text lies outside of this possibility, this reaching out of its own language. What's key is, to quote Néstor Perlongher on Wilson Bueno, "to create a minor language (in the Deleuzian sense) that mines the imposturous majesty of major languages." Thus inscribing the risk directly into the structure, as Wilson Bueno did, to make us aware of the fragility of all languages, all beings, all hearts.

Acknowledgments

Erín Moure (Canada) thanks Andrés Ajens (Chile), Christian Kent (Paraguay), Claudio Daniel (Brazil), Virna Teixeira (UK), Andrew Forster (Canada), Emma Villazón (Bolivia), Cecilia Vicuña (Chile and USA) and Stephen Motika (USA), and others for the permissions, support, and enthusiasm that permitted creation of this translation, as well as Luiz Carlos Bueno, Wilson's cousin and executor, for agreeing to its publication. Great gratitude is due as well to Odile Cisneros (Canada-Mexico-Brazil), for her close reading of and commentary on the first version, much improved, thanks to her suggestions.

I also acknowledge with thanks the University of Alberta's Department of English and Film Studies in Edmonton, Canada, where I was Writer-in-Residence in 2013-14, a position that gave me the time and financial support to complete this translation.

This work in Frenglish-ish English and Guaraní for English-language readers—this word-boat pranced and hurled giggling into the sea of all words and all shores—is dedicated to the memory of Wilson Bueno, border-crosser, enthusiast of human difference, tiller of words and magical teller of unruly tongue-tripping tales.

Credits

Excerpts of the translation have appeared in:

Oxford Book of Latin American Poetry (2009), edited Cecilia Vicuña and Ernesto Livon Grosman.

Wave Composition (2014), (wavecomposition.com)

L'Endroit indiqué (2014), (marie-anne.ca), with a further exhibition at Concordia University and catalogue (2017): created by Andrew Forster, whose visual representations of Bueno's work were hung as great strips of text, publicly on view, in and outside gallery buildings in Montreal.

The Volta, "Evening Will Come" (2015) (thevolta.org/thevolta-masthead.html), special section on translation curated and edited by Rosa Alcalá.

Asymptote, "Three Extracts from Paraguayan Sea" (July 2015) (asymptotejournal.com).

The Animated Reader, New Museum, NYC (2015).

Andrés Ajens /Sjens, Christian Kent, and Claudio Daniel, poets and editors in Chile, Paraguay, and Brazil, are again thanked, for granting permission to translate and include their texts in this volume.

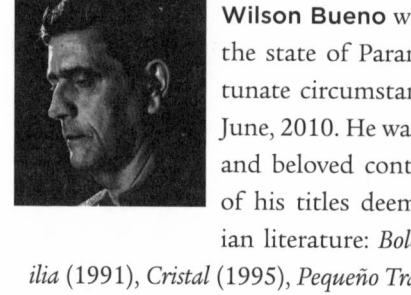

Wilson Bueno was born in 1949 in Jaguapita, in the state of Paraná in Brazil, and died in unfortunate circumstances in his home in Curitiba in June, 2010. He was one of Brazil's most influential and beloved contemporary authors, with several of his titles deemed essential to modern Brazilian literature: *Bolero's Bar* (1986), *Manual de Zoofilia* (1991), *Cristal* (1995), *Pequeño Tratado de Brinquedos* (1996), *Jardim Zoológico* (1999), *A Cavalo* (2000), *Amar-te a ti nem sei se com Carícias* (2004) and *Cachorros do Céu* (2005). Bueno's *Mar Paraguayo* (1992) is a special case, the single work by Bueno written in an admixture of three languages: Portuguese and Spanish (known as Portunhol or Portuñol) and Guaraní. *Mar Paraguayo* has already traveled across the Americas. The first edition appeared from Iluminuras, Brazil, in 1992 with a prologue by the late Néstor Perlongher. It was republished in Chile by Intemperie in 2001, and by Tsé-Tsé, Argentina, in 2005 with a luminous postface by Andrés Ajens. It was published by Bonobos in Mexico in 2006. In 2009, extracts fulminated into Frenglish/Mohawk by North-American poet and translator Erín Moure appeared in England and the USA in the *Oxford Book of Latin American Poetry* edited by Cecilia Vicuña and Ernesto Livon-Grosman. Later Moure decided that, as the text itself insisted, it was essential to keep the Guaraní. And she did. Wilson Bueno's writing has thousands of admirers in the southern realms of the Americas, and includes a cohort of multilingual mixtural South American poets a generation younger, not a "movement" but known as Yopará (or "mixturated") poets, one of whom is Christian Kent. Bueno himself encouraged Moure to translate his book, as he wished to send it on a journey through the northern Americas and other English shores not this time in its original wangling but in the mixelated accents of Quebec, moure-or-less, as *Paraguayan Sea.*

Erín Moure is a poet and translator. She has published over 30 books of poetry, essays, memoir, and translations from French, Spanish, Galician, and Portuguese. Her latest book is *Planetary Noise: Selected Poetry of Erín Moure* (Wesleyan, 2017, ed. Shannon Maguire). She lives a life of lexico-queer splendor in Montreal.

NIGHTBOAT BOOKS

Nightboat Books, a nonprofit organization, seeks to develop audiences for writers whose work resists convention and transcends boundaries. We publish books rich with poignancy, intelligence, and risk. Please visit our website, www.nightboat.org, to learn about our titles and how you can support our future publications.

The following individuals have supported the publication of this book. We thank them for their generosity and commitment to the mission of Nightboat Books:

Elizabeth Motika
Benjamin Taylor

In addition, this book has been made possible, in part, by grants from the National Endowment for the Arts and the New York State Council on the Arts Literature Program.

While we survive: even if ostrich-necked

ñanduguasú: stuck in sand: ñandu:

ñandutí: spiderweb: the crochet stitches

contorting from one to the next: corolla:

ramification of hair and ligne: slowly

announcing the fleur of flower most

florid: most nicht: ñandutimichi: almost

invisible miraculum: simulacrum: ñandy

miroir of the gods: ñandu: a thousand

t times solitaire nandini: the needle as

dark désir for blood et death: the oldie

each second ticking older: the boy: how

an they be so green, hovi mboihovi:eyes

of the boy with their myriad green flecks

hat give them color: hovi hovi hovi: my

despair bigger than the cicada-loud nuit

of the beach town of Guaratuba où I

ear myself die: maratona floozy: only